T

Incr

Book of

Vatican Facts

and

Papal

Curiosities

The
Incredible
Book of
Vatican Facts

and

Papal
Curiosities

A Treasury of Trivia

~ NINO LO BELLO ~

Liguori
LIGUORI, MISSOURI

Published by Liguori Publications
Liguori, Missouri
http://www.liguori.org

Library of Congress Cataloging-in-Publication Data

Lo Bello, Nino.
    The incredible book of Vatican facts and papal curiosities : a treasury of trivia / Nino Lo Bello. — 1st ed.
        p. cm.
    ISBN 0-7648-0171-6
    1. Popes—Miscellanea. 2. Catholic Church—Miscellanea. 3. Vatican Palace (Vatican City)—Miscellanea. I. Title.
BX957.L59   1998
262'.13—dc21   97-34251

Liguori Publications, a nonprofit corporation, is an apostolate of the Redemptorists. To learn more about the Redemptorists, visit *Redemptorists.com*.

Dedication

To my mother, Rosalia Moscarelli—a devout and devoted Sicilian mama—who, as one of the world's unheralded heroines, scrubbed each square inch of her home on her knees every single day during the disastrous flu epidemic of 1918, which killed nearly 22 million people. Her hourly prayers to Jesus and the Virgin Mary also helped to spare the family.

Acknowledgments

J ust as Pope Pius XII had his own sidekick, Sister
Pascalina, who controlled his daily life for forty years
with nary a blunder, so, too, do we owe undying
thanks to my coworker, partner-for-life, editor, and general overseer, Irene Rooney Lo Bello, whose nickname
("Lefty") does not lessen her status as my right hand. In
the preparation of this volume, twenty years or more in
the making, she has been vigilant on a day-to-day basis,
a factor that has also made possible all my other works.
Any errors, however, that may have crept into this chal-
lenging endeavor are mine.

God may also have guided my path on this one, and
to him, also, I offer my heartfelt gratitude.

—Nino Lo Bello

Foreword

Complete fascination grips visitors to Vatican City when they gaze upon St. Peter's Square and the Basilica itself, because nowhere else on Planet Three will you experience such eye-widening awe. Combinations of religious awareness and cultural wealth flow over you as you enter this tiny city-state right in the middle of Rome.

No matter how many times my husband, Nino, and I began yet another glorious adventure behind the Leonine Walls, we always did so with great anticipation. What we did not see in one day we always knew we could see another time. And we did. During the six years we lived in Rome (with our children Susan and Tom) and then the 30 years we worked in Vienna, Austria, we always went back. How else could Nino ferret out Vatican City wonders if he were not the man on the spot?

Unfortunately, Nino died shortly after finishing this manuscript, which is why I am writing the Foreword for him—but with him, nonetheless—because I feel now, and always will, his presence. Everyone who knew Nino felt his utter joy for life and his devotion to his motto, "Work hard, pray hard, play hard." With the same enthusiasm he applied to his profession, so did he also enjoy music.

In the many letters sent to me by our friends living in

far-flung places, one thought came through without fail. Never did they ever meet anyone in Nino's chosen field more able to get to the heart of a problem. And at the very same time, he could be breathless with excitement over the next performance of Verdi's *Requiem*, or the next piano recital or the upcoming summer opera season in the outdoor colosseum-look-alike arena in Verona. Nino wrote always surrounded by music; he felt himself on another level of existence and could totally block out extraneous sounds. Music was for him an inspirational, quasi-religious, experience.

For over 25 years, Nino interviewed all the opera greats for "Opera Is My Hobby," a program that still is aired on many National Public Radio stations. The founder and host of the program, Professor James Seaver, at the University of Kansas in Lawrence, Kansas, presented in Nino's honor a one-hour special memorial program during the summer of 1997, in which he played many of Nino's all-time favorites. One made Nino cry every time he listened to it and that was the *Senza Mamma* aria from Puccini's opera, *Suor Angelica.*

Another friend (a former tenor at Vienna's Staatsoper), upon hearing of Nino's unexpected death, wrote: "We miss the World's Number One Opera Fan *already!*" Others have said, "Nino probably has by this time interviewed Puccini and Verdi!"

How did Nino feel and think when he was doing research? Well, this is what he once said about that: "For me, seeking information for my articles and books has been a quixotic quest for a lot of the Old World and just enough of what is new. In seeking out the five W's of a good story, to which I wanted to add the WOW of travel, I played eeny-meeny-miney-mo with the map, traveled where Baedeker left off and poked into untrodden reaches by every known means except by oxcart and dromedary."

Now that my beloved husband and companion of 50 years is no longer with us, I must speak for him. I do believe that Nino's soul is with God, as He is with me, leading me on the path I now must take. I accept this and feel blessed that Nino and I were able to be together for half a century.

So, dear readers, I present to you Nino's last volume of work, what he had been referring to as "Vatican curioddities." I wish you as much joy with it as he had putting it all together.

—IRENE LO BELLO

Contents

Introduction

*"Trifles make perfection—
and perfection is no trifle."*
—Michelangelo (1475–1564)

It's not possible to eat one salted peanut." Back in my Brooklyn days as a kid, I heard that wise remark from a street philosopher we used to look up to as one of the Big Guys on the block (he was all of 14 years old). So I tried it many times—it never worked. And I don't know of anybody else in history who's ever eaten just one salted peanut.

What's true of the salted-peanut syndrome is true of trivia. Who can read just one trivia item without moving on to the next one, and then to the next one, and still further on to the next, the next, and the next?

And then there's the Vatican. How many people know what the pope's salary is? That is to say, how much is he paid, either monthly or annually? Next question: Does the pope have a bank account? Which gasoline brands are sold inside the state of Vatican City? Has there ever been a Jewish pope? How many rooms are there in the Apostolic Palace? What was Michelangelo's marvelous inside joke in his Sistine Chapel masterpiece, "The Last Judgment"? Does the Vatican have its own railroad station? Who was the only man to become pope three times?

What happened to Vittorio De Sica's movie that the Vatican financed and produced and never released to the public? Who indeed was Pope Joan? Has any baby ever been born in Vatican City? Which recent pope frequently talked in his sleep? Who was the only pope who was blind during most of his papacy? Are airplanes permitted to fly over Vatican City?

The answers to these questions fall into the sub-rosa realm of trivia. Yes, you'll find these particular bits of trivia—and hundreds more!—somewhere in this vast cornucopia of offbeat, oddball, unusual, fascinating, intriguing minutiae about the seat of the Roman Catholic religion (the state of Vatican City) and the people and VIPs who work there, not excluding the present occupant of Saint Peter's Throne and a few of his picturesque pontifical predecessors.

Whether you practice a religion or not—but especially if you are (as I am) one of the world's 700 million Catholics—you may have had occasion to wonder about this or that or there regarding the Vatican and those lovable news-making popes you've been reading about during your lifetime. Did any of them ever smoke? Which pope kept his own canaries? Who really designed those funny-looking uniforms worn by the Vatican's Swiss Guards? (No, it wasn't Michelangelo, and I'm not telling here—it's in the book.) To answer these intriguing questions and everything else you've always wanted to know about the Vatican but perhaps didn't know whom to ask, you have to step into my book. I'm betting that if you nibble on the first item, you'll want to devour the whole book, including the desserts awaiting you in the come-hither Appendixes. Indigestion you won't get.

Like a good meal, everything served up here is tasty. Yes, it is, after a fashion, a reference book—but a reference book you can have fun with. I have been writing about the Vatican over many years—going back to 1968, when my first book, *The Vatican Empire*, was published. A *New York Times* bestseller, that book led to my writing a quartet of other books on the Vatican. So, for almost three decades, I have been squirreling away papal trivia, seemingly insignificant Church facts, and other oddments people have been wondering about, ranging from the apostles all the way to zucchetto. No, zucchetto is not the name of an Italian cardinal lost in antiquity. So what's zucchetto? To satisfy your curiosity, you'll have to keep reading. *Buon appetito!*

The
Incredible
Book of
Vatican Facts
and
Papal
Curiosities

Chapter I

The
Papacy
and
Papal
Curiosities

Which pope holds the most "firsts"?

Besides being the first pope from Poland and the first from a Communist country, John Paul II is the first pope in anybody's memory to read without glasses. He is also the first pope to wear a wristwatch; the first pope to ski, climb mountains, and paddle a canoe; the first pope to preach in Polish from the Chair of Saint Peter; the first pope ever to repeat the names of his first three predeces-

Pope John Paul II in vestments created by the French fashion designer Jean-Charles de Castelbajac, August 1997.

3

sors; the first pope to arrive for the Conclave with only pocket money in his cassock (the equivalent of $10, all that the Polish regime would allow him to take out); the first pope in this century to sing in tune the difficult "*Ite, missa est*"; the first pope to eat a hearty breakfast of bacon and eggs instead of the traditional Italian breakfast of coffee and bread; the first pope ever to have a cocktail named after him (it includes three parts of Polish vodka); the first pope to wear vestments created for him by a prominent Paris fashion designer; the first pope under the age of 60 to be elected in over 130 years; the first Slav in history to be elected to head the Catholic Church; the first pontiff to be wounded by gunshot in public; and the first head of the Catholic Church ever to be taken to a public hospital. He is also the most traveled pope of all time.

What happens to a man when he becomes pope?

- He assumes a new name and loses most of the civil ties that bind him to his country.
- He finds his daily life regulated, often down to the most minute detail.
- He has his own confessor—who must be a Jesuit priest—who visits the Vatican once a week at a fixed time and who may absolve the pope of his sins.
- He finds that in theory he has full power over the Roman Catholic Church and every decree requires his approval. He can obey or ignore precedent. He

can set aside tradition, write or rewrite constitutions, proclaim dogmas on his own and change discipline without consultation. Although on certain matters, the pope is supposed to seek counsel and advice from the College of Cardinals, he is empowered to make up his own mind and take action. On matters of high policy, he may do as John XXIII did when, without calling in the curia cardinals for their views, he decided to go ahead with the Ecumenical Council.

- He finds he can be judged by no man. He is tantamount to a sovereign who cannot be brought to court.

The pope can do the following:

- approve or sanction or suppress religious orders
- grant indulgences
- beatify or canonize saints
- appoint bishops and name cardinals
- erect, administer, alter, or suppress bishoprics
- assign an auxiliary bishop to one who is incapacitated
- found and legislate for papal universities
- issue liturgical books
- administer the temporal goods of ecclesiastical foundations
- erect and govern missions dependent on the Holy See
- call, preside over, and adjourn ecumenical councils
- regulate holy days and Catholic feasts
- introduce new rites and abrogate old ones
- issue ex cathedra decretals on belief

- introduce or alter or suppress Church laws on any subject
- defend doctrine against heresies
- relax vows and oaths for members of religious orders who want to return to secular life
- give matrimonial dispensations
- act as a court
- establish rules of judicial procedure
- establish censures or punishments
- organize courts for hearing cases
- organize courts or appoint synodal judges for the diocese of Rome

That's what happens to a man when he becomes pope.

How long can the cardinals take to elect a pope?

There is no time-limit rule governing the election of a new pope at a Conclave. The longest time needed in Vatican history to come up with a new pope came when the reign of Pope Clement IV ended in the year 1268. It took the assembled cardinals 2 years, 9 months, and 2 days—and on September 1, 1271, one Teobaldo Visconti became Pope Gregory X.

Which pope died on an island and in exile?

Pope Saint Silverius, who reigned from June 536 to November 537, is the only pontiff to have died on an island. Having been installed by the Goths, he was violently unseated by the militant Byzantine Empress Theodora and banished to the Island of Ponza off Italy's Mediterranean coast. Today he is the patron saint of the isle, and there is a feast in his honor every year during the month of June. It goes on for several days and gathers momentum as distant guns proclaim the approach of an illuminated vessel, attended by a flotilla of smaller lit-up boats, when they come into view around the headland of the village of Santa Maria.

How does John Paul II keep up with the news?

A team of priests assigned to the Vatican Secretariat of State prepares a daily digest of events from around the world. About 30 newspapers from Italy and other countries are read, and articles are clipped, summarized, and translated into Italian each morning. This digest runs about 20 pages and is presented to the pope around 10 o'clock in the morning. Although there is a television set in an office near the pope's, John Paul does not look at television news. Since he reads English, he often peruses daily copies of the *International Herald Tribune* and is a fan of the Art Buchwald column.

Has a pope ever been sued successfully?

Newspapers had a field day when a California law student, William Sheffield, sued Pope Paul VI for the sum of $428.50 because a Swiss monastery did not deliver the newborn Saint Bernard dog he had purchased. Headlines at the time read:

- Pope Loses Pip of a Suit Over a Pup
- Vatican Is Dogmatic in Court
- Pup, 1, Pope 0

An attorney in Santa Ana, Mr. Sheffield goes down in Vatican history as the only person ever to have sued a pope. He also goes down as the only person to have sued a pope successfully, because an Alameda County superior court judge awarded him a $428.50 default judgment against Paul VI on the grounds that he never received delivery of the puppy, for which he had paid a $60 deposit to a Roman Catholic monk in Switzerland. In his suit, which took some six years of litigation, Sheffield named the Roman Catholic Church and the pope as ultimately responsible for the Church's business obligations.

Although he won the suit, Sheffield has never been able to collect.

Do popes make public appearances in frigid weather?

Pope John Paul II does. With Europe undergoing a severe freeze and gusty winds, he appeared for his usual Sunday blessing on December 29, 1996, holding tight to his papal cap as the hardy visitors in St. Peter's Square endured the record-breaking cold weather. Said the pope: "I hope you are courageous in the face of the cold. Warm yourselves up. It seems that today you can hear the wind more than the pope." The pontiff noted that temperatures had dipped as low as 35 degrees below zero in Poland.

What is John Paul II's nickname?

His nickname is Lolek, which was given to him during his childhood. It is still used by his family and close Polish friends.

Who was Pope John XX?

Pope John XX never was. To correct an error in sequence in the tenth century, the Vatican passed over "John XX." The name John has been the most popular (and unlucky) of all papal names. Altogether, there were 22 Pope Johns—the last one being Pope John XXIII. Before him, no pope had taken the John name for almost seven centuries, probably because of the misfortune associated with the name in Vatican history. For instance: Pope John VII was killed by members of his family in 882. Deposed, Pope John XI died in prison in 935. John XII was beaten to death by the irate husband of a woman suspected of being a papal mistress.

Which pope was exhumed for a public trial?

Only one pope in history ever stood public trial—and it happened nine months after his death! In one of the most macabre episodes in history, Pope Formosus's body was exhumed in March 897 and dressed in papal vestments. Charged with usurping the papal throne, he was found guilty. The body was forthwith stripped of its pontifical vestments, and the fingers of his right hand (used for papal blessings) were chopped off. Then Formosus's remains were thrown into the Tiber River.

Has a pope ever been impeached?

The Vatican's official list of popes of the past does not include the name of Pope John XXIII—the one who reigned from 1410 to 1415. Having chosen the name of John XXIII (the same one that Cardinal Angelo Roncalli took when elected to succeed Pius XII on October 25, 1958), Baldassare Cossa was named pope on May 25, 1410. This followed the death of Alexander V, who had been chosen by the Council of Pisa as a rival to the then-reigning Pope Gregory XII (Angelo Correr of Venice [1406–1415]).

Known as a schismatic pope, Cossa—having become politically embroiled with Emperor Sigismund—was deposed by a decree of the Council of Constance. The first Pope John XXIII was considered "an embarrassment" and was officially booted out of office for "notorious incest, adultery, defilement and homicide," together with the discovery that his mistress was his brother's wife. To keep the pope's scandalous behavior from becoming public, John XXIII was sent to Tusculum, where he served as a cardinal-bishop for four years, during which time he was reputed to have seduced more than 200 nuns, maidens, married women, and widows.

What is an antipope?

By definition an "antipope" was a man who sat on the papal throne but whose election was eventually declared uncanonical. Antipopes came about as a result of different types of historical situations—such as doctrinal disagreements, deportation of a legitimate pope (exile), a double election, or political instabilities of the era. From the year 217 until 1449 there were nearly 40 antipopes who endeavored to, or actually did, win the papacy in opposition to someone else chosen as pontiff.

Whenever the Catholic Church had an antipope, it was difficult for contemporaries to decide who was the true pope. Among history's more important antipopes were Felix II, Clement III, Anacletus II, Nicholas V, Clement VII, Benedict XIII, John XXIII (Baldassare Cossa), and Felix V, who served from 1439–1449 as the last antipope.

Why does John Paul II travel with containers of blood?

Whenever he goes on one of his trips abroad, the Vatican's most traveled pope, John Paul II, brings along bottles of blood taken from his own body. John Paul II has a rare blood type, and in case of an emergency Vatican officials do not want to depend on foreign blood banks.

What is the funniest anecdote told about John XXIII?

An anecdote still making the rounds long after his death was the perennial favorite about Pope John XXIII.

As the story goes, soon after his coronation in 1958, his relatives visited the Apostolic Palace for the first time. A papal audience is an impressive experience for most people, and John's folks were no exception. Having walked timidly through the golden halls, past the omnipresent Swiss Guards, they dropped to their knees and bowed their heads when they saw John dressed in his splendiferous pontifical white robes.

"Forget all that!" said John. "What are you afraid of? It's only me!"

Has there ever been a Jewish pope?

The first pope, Saint Peter, was, like all of the original twelve disciples, born into a Jewish family and raised a Jew. Aside from him, there has been one other pope of Jewish heritage. In 1130, a majority of cardinals put into office a fellow cardinal whose great-grandfather had been a Jew. Anacletus II came from a family which had converted to Christianity, starting with a prominent Jewish leader of the Middle Ages by the name of Baruch. Accepting the faith of Christ, Baruch changed his name to Benedictus—the literal translation into Latin of the meaning of Baruch, "blessed."

Baruch's son, Leo de Benedicto Cristiano—literally, son of Baruch the Christian—was one of the wealthiest men in Rome in the mid-eleventh century. Leo's son, Petrus Leonis, then headed the Pierleoni Family, which kept its powerful status in Rome during the early twelfth century, and although it failed twice to get one of its members selected to the papacy, it succeeded the third time in 1130 with Anacletus II. But his election was later declared uncanonical, and he was eventually termed an "antipope." Opinion was then and still is divided among scholars as to where the precise canonical right lay, since there was some doubtful legality involving both sides at the time.

As the first and only pope of Jewish heritage in Vatican history since Saint Peter, Anacletus II had his share of enemies, a phenomenon of the Middle Ages shared by every pope. In the case of Anacletus, the Church was torn asunder when a minority faction of cardinals elected a Roman to the Throne of Saint Peter—Innocent II. To shore up his shaky position, Anacletus sought and got the military backing of Sicily's King Roger II. By a bull signed at Avellino in September 1130, Anacletus invested Roger with the kingdom of Sicily, Calabria, and Apulia, the principality of Capua, and the fief of Naples, in return for acknowledging the Holy See's feudal suzerainty and the payment of an annual tribute.

After this political maneuver on the part of Anacletus, Innocent was forced to leave Rome and head for France, there to be accepted as the official pope by Bernard de Clairvaux (later Saint Bernard)—one of Europe's most influential ecclesiastical leaders. De Clairvaux began a campaign to blacken the name of Pope Anacletus II by vigorous invective, calling him "Anacletus the Jew Pope," and even accusing him of having an incestuous relationship with his sister. Anacletus's ancestors had a good name both as Jews and Christians, but the campaign against him grew more and more vicious, as the power-hungry men within the Church were not necessarily influenced by theosophical ideals but by worldly goods. Nevertheless, Anacletus's enemies never succeeded in unseating him—and in January 1138 the "Jewish" pope died.

Which pope did his own typing?

Pope Pius XII was the only pope who knew how to use a typewriter. Virtually up to the time he fell fatally ill, he typed most of his own speeches, not to mention the first drafts to many of his encyclicals.

What was John Paul II's first near-miss with death?

Pope John Paul II came very close to death while a boy. Hit by a truck in Poland, he lay alongside the road until found the next morning. He suffered a fractured skull.

Does Pope John Paul II get more of one kind of mail than any other head of state?

Yes, indeed—letters from children. Certain ones so tickle the pontiff that he saves them in a file. Some examples:

> Dear Pope, you are different. I like hearing about the popes before you but I like you the best. Do you think you could reform the world since your predecessors did not finish the task? (from a 14-year-old)

> You who are the deputy of Jesus should tell Jesus to put an end to purse-snatching, to put an end to wars and to put an end to all

kidnappings because all these are sins. (from an 8-year-old)

I saw you on the television before that bad man shot you. It must be a hard world for you to live in, exposed to danger that way. I know that Jesus will make you better soon. Spaghetti is good for the health, and if you eat it more often instead of Polish dishes, you will get better faster. Take my advice! (from a 10-year-old)

Dear Pope John Paul: What is it like when you die? Nobody will tell me. I just want to know, but I don't want to do it. (from an 11-year-old)

The pope has even received some telegrams, the best of which (from a boy of 14) reads like this:

When I go to sleep at night, I have dreams, and sometimes they are bad and frighten me. Please, can you have God send better movies every night? I like Robin Williams.

The funniest message, according to a papal office secretary, is the one from a little girl (age 9) in Boston:

Holy Sir, my mother told me that when I was born, the stork brought me. Then when my

brother was born, the stork also brought him.
Dear Pope, can you arrange it with God for
my mother to have a normal birth the next
time?

One letter (from a 10-year-old author) arrived addressed actually to "God, in care of The Pope," which read:

Here I am, O Jesus mine, I read your book.
Next time you write a Bible, put a lot of zip in
it.

What does John Paul II's handwriting say about him?

Curious as to what an analysis of his handwriting might reveal, Pope John Paul II had a sample of it submitted to one of Italy's top graphologists, who was not told the calligraphy belonged to the pope. The report came back after a few days, and John Paul II had some fun reading about himself. The report stated that the one characteristic that stood out in the handwriting was a genuine fondness for people and love for unpretentious things. The script leaned to the right, said the analysis, which showed the person had deep warmth for others. "The person is a deliberate man and has a fondness for details, judging from the way he dots his *i*'s very close to the letters. The space between the words tells us of yet another side to the person's complex character. He needs sometimes to be alone and contemplate things because he relishes periods of isolation from time to time." The report added that the man in question had a real sense of humor and also a temper, which he was not afraid to vent. Finally the graphologist also pointed out that the subject was a remarkable man.

Which pope is memorialized at Loreto?

Dominating a ridge and surrounded by massive brick ramparts with large rounded towers, the sanctuary of Loreto is 18 miles southeast of Ancona on Italy's Adriatic coast. Three major pilgrimages to Loreto are held each

Photo by Nino Lo Bello

Statue of Pope John XXIII at the sanctuary of Loreto.

year—one in March, one in August, and another in December. In 1965, Pope John XXIII personally led a pilgrimage to Loreto, and a giant statue in honor of him has been erected near "the Holy House," which, according to Catholic history, was carried from Nazareth to Loreto in 1294. Also notable are the frescoes at Loreto, created by Luca Signorelli in 1479 and among the finest in the world. Signorelli, a Renaissance painter who did the *Testament of Moses* in the Sistine Chapel, had a decided influence on the work of Michelangelo.

Has there ever been a married pope?

At one time in Church history popes did not have to be unmarried. Saint Peter was married, and the Bible even mentions his mother-in-law, who was healed by Jesus. One pope, Hormisdas (514–523) was the father of Pope Silverius (536–537). Reigning from 590 to 604, Pope Gregory I (also known as Pope Gregory the Great) was the great-grandson of Pope Felix III (483–492).

Hadrian II (867–872), before becoming pope, was married and had a daughter. Lame and blind in one eye, Pope Hadrian did not want to give up his family or become celibate, so—amid criticism—he kept his wife and daughter with him in the Lateran Palace. Unknown persons abducted the pope's wife and child, which prompted Hadrian to petition for police help and military support from Emperor Louis II of France. No sooner had Louis agreed to do so than the kidnappers promptly murdered the pope's wife and daughter. The culprits were never apprehended.

Where does John Paul II swim?

Pope John Paul II (shown here addressing a Sunday morning gathering of the faithful from the balcony of the papal summer residence at Castel Gandolfo) has a glass-and-concrete swimming pool at his disposal inside the palace grounds. The pope's watery playpen is more than just a swimming pool, for it includes a sauna, solarium, and gymnasium. Because the pool itself is Olympic size (182 feet long), John Paul gives himself a

Photo by: Nino Lo Bello

Pope John Paul II greets pilgrims from the balcony of the Castel Gandolfo summer residence.

good workout during a swim. John Paul's desire to take a dip is not to practice his natatory navigation so much as it is to obey his doctor's orders to do so. Though he doesn't show it, he suffers from a spinal ailment (known as anckylosing spondylitis), which makes him tend to be round-shouldered, and the recommended therapy is to swim on his back. (See page 166 for more details on the popes' summer palace.)

Why is there a papal palace in France?
The mammoth palace of the popes in Avignon, a one-hour train ride north of Marseille, is a soaring fortress that served as a home and refuge for seven pontiffs and

Papal palace in Avignon, France.

as the seat of the "second Vatican" during the fourteenth century, when rival factions tore the city of Rome apart and forced the pontiffs to seek refuge in a more hospitable land, the south of France. With the exception of one very brief interval, the popes lived in the lofty structure from 1309 to 1376, when they finally ended their self-imposed exile and returned to Rome.

Avignon was a convenient place for the Church hierarchy to live, especially after Pope Benedict XII had built the massive palace that still dominates the town. A seat of luxury and magnificence, the Avignon Palace fell into decay as a result of the French Revolution, so that today the building is almost denuded of its murals and ornaments. Some former elegance can be seen with professional guides in the so-called Wardrobe Tower and the Papal Bedchamber (with painted birdcages and blue-and-yellow birds), miraculously rescued from the fury of the mobs.

Which pope was insulted by an artist?

The most lasting colossal insult ever heaped on any pope is still very visible today in Rome. If you approach the Porta Pia Square from the Via XX Settembre, you will notice three white reliefs to the right, left, and in the center of the arch. Though they look like generic ornamentations, they are in reality shaving bowls with a piece of soap inside, each draped with a fringed towel. The artist who created them did not like Pope Pius IV, who had ordered the arch to be built in 1546 following a design submitted by Michelangelo. The subtle joke of the three barbers' bowls was a wry reference to the humble background of the pope, whose ancestors were barbers. This amusing baroque trifle did not come to the attention of the Vatican until almost a century later.

Photo by Nino Lo Bello

The arch at Porta Pia Square showing 3 shaving bowls with soap and fringed towels.

What was John XXIII's favorite pastime?

Pope John XXIII liked to hide out in Vatican City's tallest building (known as the Tower of the Winds), which had a penthouse apartment consisting of eight rooms and a terrace. Armed with a pair of binoculars, he would spend a relaxing hour or so observing what was happening on the streets of Rome—whether it was housewives hang-

Tower of the Winds: Vatican City's tallest building.

ing out the weekly laundry or children playing on the streets. The Tower of the Winds is today used by the Vatican to house distinguished visitors. It was also used by John Paul II while extensive repairs were being made to his quarters in the Apostolic Palace.

What are some of the pope's other titles?

The papal office is not without its array of titles—official and unofficial. Officially, the pope is the Bishop of Rome, Successor of the Prince of Apostles, Vicar of Jesus Christ, Supreme Pontiff of the Universal Church, Servant of the Servants of God, Patriarch of the West, Primate of Italy, Archbishop and Metropolitan of the Roman Province, and Sovereign of the State of Vatican City. Unofficially, he is often called Rector of the World upon Earth, Father of Princes and Kings, and Pontifex Maximus. The last name is usually seen in abbreviated form, as Pont. Max.

How did Queen Victoria address the pope?

The Vatican Archives contain a letter from Queen Victoria that shows that she did not want to acknowledge any of the papal titles. Her letter to the pope began with "Most Eminent Sir" instead of the usual "Your Holiness." In his reply, however, Pope Leo XIII addressed Victoria as "The Most Serene and Powerful Victoria, Queen of the United

Kingdom of Great Britain and Ireland and Other Regions, Illustrious Empress of India."

Which pope wore a hairshirt under his ceremonial dress?

Pope Paul VI, who had the build of a professional wrestler, wore a hairshirt studded with metal points that scratched the skin on his chest during much of his adult life. He began wearing the odd garment from time to time as a young priest, and after being elected to the papacy in 1963, he wore the hairshirt underneath his rich robes on every important occasion, despite the fact that the metal points pressed hard against his flesh and sometimes drew blood.

Which pope was a wine connoisseur?

Believing that wine was not only good for digestion but also important for one's health as a medicine, Pope Pius XII drank at least one glass of wine every day he was in office; on trips he carried a personal flask under his papal robes.

Has a pope ever been murdered?

At least one pope—John XII—was murdered. He was elected pope on December 16, 955, at the age of 18. He was murdered on December 4, 963.

What is the pope's salary?

When a ranking cardinal wins an election to the Seat of Saint Peter, he earns, in effect, a promotion—but with a reduction in pay to zero. Incredible but true: The Holy Father receives not a penny in pay. Also astonishing: The pope does not have a bank account.

Which pope gave his name to a popular egg dish?

Eggs Benedict got its name from Pope Benedict XIII, who favored this dish for breakfast during the years he reigned (1724–1730).

Which pope was solicitous of insects?

Pope Pius XII did not like the idea of stepping on any kind of insect. And so, during the walks he took in the papal gardens on almost every afternoon of his pontificate, the gardeners—unknown to the pope—kept his path clear by spraying insecticide ahead of time. Had he known of this stratagem, Pius XII would indeed have been miffed.

Which pope's remains were disturbed by grave robbers?

After lying unmolested for more than 450 years, the remains of Saint Celestine V (the only pope to resign his office) were stolen from an urn in a church in Aquila, Italy, in April 1988. After a day and a half they were found by the police in a cemetery in the village of Amatrice, not very far away.

What is the legend about Pope Saint Gregory as an author?

Pope Saint Gregory the Great (590–604) dictated all his books to a scribe from behind a curtain. Inside the Vatican there is a fresco of Pope Gregory that depicts a legend about him: At one time when the pope was doing his dictation, a secretary pulled the curtain aside and saw the Holy Spirit in the form of a dove close to his ear, whispering to him what to say in his new book.

Which pope gave an audience to an eel?

The tale of the eel that one day left its home in Lake Bracciano, some 50 miles outside Rome, and swam all the way to Vatican City to make an unscheduled "appearance" underneath the pope's window has every earmark of a fish story—and yet it happened.

The eel apparently slithered into one of the water pipes leading to Rome and to the Vatican and ended up stuck inside one of the two famed fountains in St. Peter's Square, just below the papal chambers. Pope Pius XII glanced out the window and noticed to his bewilderment that there was no water in the fountain. At breakfast he commented to his housekeeper on how odd it was that there was water gushing from the far fountain but not from "our fountain." Sister Pasqualina (the Italianized version of her name) picked up the phone and called the fire department. The firemen arrived, as did a number of journalists, and when the fountain's innards were examined, the eel was found. Once the eel was removed from the tiny pipe in which it had been lodged, the fountain came to life again—and the eel was carried away in a pail.

Which recent pope frequently talked in his sleep?

Pope John XXIII reputedly talked in his sleep a lot. Reports from the Vatican say that he often dreamed about his problems. He was once overheard to murmur, while napping: "I don't know. I will have to ask the pope."

Who was the last pope to host a papal banquet?

Above all, Pope Pius IX loved to give big banquets and was actually the last pope to do so. He even gave one banquet outdoors on the roof of St. Peter's, to which 300 guests were invited. The menu consisted of ten courses and five different wines. After the meal was finished and the guests adjourned to the papal gardens

Pope Pius IX who proclaimed the Immaculate Conception of the Blessed Virgin as dogma and who convened the First Vatican Council.

below for coffee, the some hundred waiters and bus-
boys fell on all the remaining food and even ate up
what was left on the pope's plate. On one occasion in
1863, the pope gave a dinner for several hundred of
Rome's beggars.

Which pope had a "kidnapping" in his past?

While Cardinal Roncalli (later Pope John XXIII) was the
patriarch of Venice, he hosted a distinguished guest from
Poland, Cardinal Wyszynski, who had just been released
from prison by the regime. Wyszynski's train had a 45-
minute layover at Venice (on its way to Rome), and
Roncalli suggested to his visitor that they take a quick
sightseeing tour of Venice by motorboat. The Polish cardinal, thrilled by the beauty of the Grand Canal, failed
to notice that more than three-quarters of an hour had
gone by, and when he did, he groaned. "Good heavens,
my train has left!" Roncalli calmly told him not to worry,
adding, "Do you see that man sitting at the back of our
boat? He's the engineer of your train. I kidnapped him,
and while he is with us, your train cannot leave the
station."

Does John Paul II bowl?

Although John Paul II is a dedicated sportsman who skis
well, swims regularly in his summer-home pool, and does

a lot of hiking, he has never once used the bowling alley that Pope John XXIII put in for Vatican use.

Which pope was vetoed by an emperor?

The Austrian Empire (1804–1918) claimed many of the rights of the Holy Roman Empire—such as the right to veto the election of a pope. In 1903 Emperor Franz Josef made use of this right. Though the most likely candidate, Cardinal Rampolla's election was vetoed by the emperor because his people considered Rampolla to be too hostile to Austria. Cardinal Giuseppe Sarto was then elected to the papacy, and he took the name of Pius X. Immediately after his election, Pius X abolished Austria's privilege of veto once and for all.

Why did John Paul II refuse an inheritance?

In 1981 Pope John Paul II refused to be the beneficiary to a will that left him over $2 million when an elderly clairvoyant in Piacenza—known throughout central Italy as "Mamma Rosa"—died and left her estate to him. Rosa Buzzini Quattrini, who for 17 years collected money from people who went to her to have their fortunes told, claimed she had seen the Madonna in a vision. The Vatican had studied her case and concluded she had not had the vision and had forbidden Catholics to seek her services as an intermediary to the Virgin Mary.

Does John Paul II have any American relatives?

The Polish pope has one direct relative in the United States—a cousin in Detroit, John E. Wojtyla—who sends a Christmas card each year. The pope himself, though more concerned with the spiritual side of Christmas, does give presents to some friends (he has no immediate family in Poland) and to everyone who works in the Vatican, from the lowliest street sweepers to the most distinguished cardinals—a bottle of sparkling spumante wine and a panettone (a golden yeast cake studded with raisins and citron), which is the traditional loaf in Italy.

Which pope had a problem pronouncing "Helsinki"?

Just before President Kekkonen of Finland was to call on Pope Paul VI in 1975, the ambassador to the Holy See made a formal preliminary visit to the Vatican to work out certain protocol procedures. Since Paul kept mispronouncing the word "Helsinki" (he said "Helsinski"), the envoy discreetly corrected the pope's pronunciation. To make sure he would get it right, the pope said it three times in a row. On the occasion of Kekkonen's arrival, Paul again made the same mistake, calling the Finnish capital "Helsinski." Then he turned to the ambassador and said proudly, "There, I did get it right this time, didn't I?"

How did the pope become a promoter of women's millinery?

In the spring of 1958, the Vatican became the victim of a "hat trick" carried out by an aggressive PR man, Guido Orlando, who had been hired by the Millinery Institute of America to promote the sale of women's hats. He accomplished this by involving Pope Pius XII.

Knowing that Vatican rules required women to cover their heads at church, Orlando got the pope to make an official declaration stating that hats were a proper part of women's dress. On a phony letterhead (titled Religious Research Institute), Orlando told the pope a falsehood: that a survey showed that over 20 million women in North America attended Mass every week without their heads covered. Boldly, Orlando suggested in his letter several sentences that could be used by the pope: "Of the various pieces of apparel worn by women today, hats do the most to enhance the dignity and decorum of womanhood. It is traditional for hats to be worn by women in church and other religious occasions— and I commend hats as a right and proper part of women's dress."

Shortly after receiving Orlando's letter, Pope Pius incorporated these very words into a general recommendation that women wear hats, and it was published by *L'Osservatore Romano* and picked up by the wire services. Within a month there was a sharp upturn in the sale of women's hats.

Has there ever been a playwright pope?

John Paul II is the author of four books and over 500 articles and essays. In 1960, his play *The Jeweler's Shop*, a trilogy about marriage, was published under the pseudonym of Andrzej Jawien. In subsequent years the play has been broadcast over the radio in many countries, presented in London on the stage, and done as a TV movie with Burt Lancaster.

Which popes held down lay jobs before entering the priesthood?

Pope Eusebius (A.D. 310) was a medical doctor and a professional historian. Pope Boniface VIII (1294–1303) was a practicing lawyer. Pope Pius II (1458–1464) was a novelist and a poet laureate. Pope Innocent X (1644–1655) was a presiding judge, and Pope Innocent XI (1676–1689) was a banker.

How does a pope get elected?

Elections for a new pope come about when the pope in office dies, but these elections are like no other in the world. Moreover, the results are presented to the world in a most unusual fashion. When all the cardinals have congregated for the voting, the meeting takes place in none other than the world-renowned Sistine Chapel. And the cardinals make the results of each ballot known by burning straw or paper—straw makes black smoke and paper creates white smoke—which tells the thousands of people waiting outside in St. Peter's Square whether or not a pope has been elected. From a little chimney inside the Sistine Chapel, the smoke puffs out from a spot in front of the gable to the right of the facade of the basilica. Two ballots are cast each day. If the smoke comes out black, no new pope has been elected.

If the smoke is white, a pope has indeed been elected, and the highest-ranking cardinal emerges on the middle loggia and announces the name of the newly elected pope to the crowds assembled below. Then the new pontiff emerges in a white cassock and gives his first papal blessing, *Urbi et Orbi* (which means "To the City and to the World").

Who was the only man to become pope three times?

Pope Benedict IX (1032–1044), who first became pope at the age of 14, was the only man to be pope three times. The first time he abdicated was to marry. After returning as pope for a second period in office, he abdicated for a second time when he sold his papal seat to his godfather. Then he became pope again. All this took place before Benedict reached the age of 30.

Has a pope ever written a cookbook?

The only pope who ever wrote a cookbook was Pope Pius V (1566–1572), who compiled *The Cooking Secrets of Pope Pius V*. His favorite dessert was quince tart, which he included in the papal cookbook.

Monument to Pope Pius V in the Basilica of St. Mary Major, Rome.

Which pope wrote a letter to an imaginary character?

Pope John Paul I, who died 34 days after being in office, once wrote an affectionate fan letter to Pinocchio, the text of which is available in a collection of his letters.

Which pope was an automobile buff?

Pius XI (1922–1939) kept a fleet of 16 cars in the Vatican garage. Three of these were convertibles.

Which recent pope was a smoker?

Pope Paul VI (1963–1978) was known, at times, to smoke as much as a pack a day. Pope Pius XII was for many years a user of snuff but gave it up after recovering from pneumonia.

Has a pope ever been born out of wedlock?

Only two illegitimate children ever reached the papal throne: Pope John XI, who reigned from March 931 to December 935, and Clement VII, a member of the Medici family who stayed in office from November 1523 to September 1534.

Who was the "Warrior Pope"?

Only one pope ever went to war. Known as the "Warrior Pope," Pope Julius II (1503–1513), dressed in a full suit of armor, led his Crusade troops into battle on several occasions. Admired for his fighting prowess, he was known as *"Il Terribile"* ("The Terrible One"). When Michelangelo fashioned a statue of Pope Julius, seated with a book in his hands, the pope asked the artist to remove the book and replace it with a sword.

Pope Julius II was chiefly a soldier, and his fame was due to his restoration of the temporal power of the papacy and to his deliverance of Italy from occupation by French troops.

39

What was the joke played on Pius XI by a group of children?

Pope Pius XI frequently allowed the children of Vatican employees to play in the gardens. One day, speaking to the youngsters as they watched a school of flashy red fish swimming in one of the ponds, he said, "So many cardinals—and no pope!" The next day two giggling boys and a girl went to the pond and emptied the contents of a pail into it. When Pius went out for his usual stroll, he saw one fish that stood out from all the others. The fish was all white—just like the pope's robes.

What impresses people most about John Paul II?

When an Indiana diocesan newspaper sponsored an essay contest asking readers to write what impressed them most about Pope John Paul II, nearly 450 people responded. Numerically, what impressed them the most were his smile, his devotion to Mary, his fluency in foreign languages, his forgiveness of his would-be assassin, and his love for children. Many people said they liked his gesture of kissing the ground upon arriving in a country.

Are popes made up for their TV appearances?

When he appeared on television for the very first time, Pope Pius XII (1939–1958) had his face "restored" with pancake makeup. Since that time, the practice of television makeup for papal faces was wisely abandoned.

Which pope announced his own election to his fellow cardinals?

In the Conclave June 1846, following the death of Pope Gregory XVI, Cardinal Giovanni Maria Mastai Ferretti had the job of calling out the votes cast for the various papal candidates. During the third ballot he found himself reading out his own name 18 times. Nervous and not sure whether he could continue, the shocked cardinal was prevailed upon to continue carrying out his duty. He went on to read his own name 36 times, which comprised the necessary two-thirds majority to elect him pope. He took the name Pope Pius IX and served until his death 32 years later.

Which pope had a pet named Gretchen?

Gretchen was the name of Pope Pius XII's favorite canary. Let out of her cage every morning, the bird hopped onto the pontiff's arm (sometimes on his shoulder) and then flew over to the breakfast table to peck at whatever breadcrumbs were still there.

What was Pius XII's reaction to the liberation of Rome from the Nazis?

One of the few witty remarks attributed to Pope Pius XII came on the day American troops entered Rome during World War II for the first time, driving out the Nazi defenders to the north. When Major General E. N. Harmon offered apologies for the excruciating noises the rumbling GI tanks had made, Pius XII said with a smile: "Anytime one liberates Rome, he has the right to make all the noise he likes."

Which modern pope came from an impoverished background?

Popes have had varying amounts of personal wealth, but probably no pope has had as little as Pope John XXIII. Before he assumed the papal throne, Cardinal Roncalli managed to accumulate enough money for his family to buy back the house in which he and his brothers had been born so that the Roncalli clan could once again live under the same roof. Dr. Piero Mazzoni, the Roman physician who attended Pope John in his dying days, discovered that a fountain pen was one of John's very few personal possessions of value.

"Take this pen," whispered the pontiff to his doctor on his deathbed. "It's all I have with which to repay you for your care and devotion. It's almost new, for I've hardly ever used it." The only other possession John left behind was his pectoral cross, which he gave to Franz Cardinal Koenig, then the archbishop of Vienna, who wore it at special events.

Which pope was an ex-con?

Found guilty of having started a fight in church on the sabbath, a man who was later to become Pope Callistus (217–222) worked in the salt mines of Sardinia as a convict for a year.

Was there ever a bed-ridden pope?

Two years after taking office, Pope Clement XII (1730–1740) was blinded. He also spent most of his ten years in office in bed with a severe case of gout.

Which pope was a speed demon?

Pope Paul VI loved speed. While the archbishop of Milan, he used to speed around the countryside in the fastest car that was available to him. Later, as pope in Rome, he often sat in the back of his limousine with a stopwatch, fervently urging his chauffeur to drive still faster.

Which pope lived in a cave before being elected pope?

While living in a cave as a monk, Celestine V was named pope after he wrote a letter of complaint urging the Vatican to name a pontiff because, thanks to a power struggle, there had not been a pope for two years. Before one year was up, Pope Celestine resigned his papacy. His successor, Boniface VIII, imprisoned Celestine in the castle at Fumone.

Did a pope ever lose his temper in public?

The only time that the affable Pope John XXIII was ever seen to lose his temper in public came when he was about to make a short talk and a Vatican garden worker began to remove some palms nearby. Pope John asked the man to leave the palms where they were, but the man ignored him and kept working at the removal of the palms. The pope asked him again, and still the man went on with his work, oblivious to the pontiff. Plainly miffed, Pope John flailed both arms at the worker and ordered him out, using some choice words of Venetian dialect.

How does one get to see the pope?

How to see the pope is a question every tourist to Rome asks. And the only answer is, it depends. If you want to attend a general papal audience, then equip yourself beforehand with a letter from a bishop in your hometown or home state, or even from any priest in Rome. The pope holds general audiences during most of the year when he is in residence in the Vatican. On Wednesdays there is an audience around noontime in the Aula della Udienze (now named after Pope Paul VI), which can accommodate some 6,000 people. One way to get tickets to this audience is to go to the American Catholic Church in Rome (St. Susanna) at Via XX Settembre 14— or go to the North American College (the national college for American seminarians and priests in Rome), where tickets are available for as long as the supply lasts. All tickets are free.

When the pope is at his summer residence in Castel Gandolfo (during August and part of September), he gives a general audience in a large assembly hall on Wednesdays at noon, for which tickets can be arranged at the Vatican Tourist Office in St. Peter's Square.

If you just want to see the pope, he appears at his window in the Apostolic Palace overlooking St. Peter's Square every Sunday morning at noon to give his blessing (top floor, second window from the right). The same goes for Castel Gandolfo when he gives his Sunday blessing from the residence balcony to some 7,000 to 10,000 people.

What is a papal funeral like?

The funeral of a pope is governed by strict formal procedures. First, the body must be officially identified by the cardinal chamberlain, and the Ring of the Fisherman must be removed from the pontiff's finger and broken up into small bits. Forthwith, a long procession consisting of cardinals and other Vatican notables escort him to the Sistine Chapel, where the body is then dressed in special clothing consisting of white silk and specially woven pallium. Gloves are put on the dead pope, and a golden miter is placed on his head. The body of the deceased pontiff is then placed in any one of several chapels in the Apostolic Palace. On the next day, his body is carried into St. Peter's, where he lies in state for three days as interminable crowds pass by for a last visit. If the funeral Mass is held inside St. Peter's, it takes place at the Altar of the Chair. Next, the body is laid in a triple casket of polished wood. A Latin eulogy of the deeds of the deceased pope is then read and laid at his feet, enclosed in a brass cylinder. Three red velvet bags of gold, silver, and copper coins (one for each year of his reign) are placed beside him. Then the pope's face is covered with a silk veil, just before the triple casket is closed and sealed. Finally, the pontifical casket is lowered into the crypt.

For which pope did Italian workers break a strike?

For an important ceremony in St. Peter's during the reign of Pope John XXIII, the Vatican needed additional electric power, because TV and radio units required a minimum load of 3,500 kilowatts. (Vatican generators provide a maximum of 2,100 kilowatts.) Since the electrical workers in Rome were on strike, the Vatican secretary of state appealed to them to provide at least enough power for the Basilica. The answer came back from the union leader: "Yes! For Pope John we will do it. He has brought light to us. We will give some back to him."

Are there any restrictions of nationality on the papacy?

Although a pope can be a man of any nationality, the men elected so far have been Syrians, Greeks, Frenchmen, Spaniards, one Portuguese, one Englishman, one Pole, and a large number of Italians.

What was the pope's plan to outwit Hitler?

Tipped off that Adolf Hitler had laid plans to arrest him and remove him from the Vatican, Pope Pius XII prepared a written resignation that was signed and notarized—so that he would not be the pope or Pope Pius XII when escorted by German soldiers beyond the walls of the State of Vatican City. Instead he would simply be a private Italian citizen called Eugenio Pacelli, his baptismal name. In that way the Church would not plunge into a crisis similar to the one that occurred in the late eighteenth century when French forces seized Pope Pius VI—in which case the Church would have had to await his death in captivity before restoring its government.

Which pope had a precocious sense of vocation?

Pope Benedict XV (1914–1922) played priest as a little boy when his grandmother gave him a toy altar for Christmas.

Which pope almost lost his life in the Vatican Library?

Pius XI once had a narrow escape from death in the Vatican Library on December 22, 1931. Ten minutes after he had completed a business visit to the library, the roof of the room he had been in for a half hour crashed through the floor and on down to the basement. One person was killed—the priest with whom the pope had been conferring.

How many popes have been accomplished linguists?

The only pope who can be truly called a linguist is Pope John Paul II. Besides his mother tongue, Polish, John

Paul II can converse (without the aid of a dictionary) in Italian, French, English, German, and Spanish. His fluency in Latin is considered perfect by the Latinists inside the Vatican. John Paul also has a working knowledge of Japanese and Tagalog and is familiar with several African dialects.

How did a pope get the better of Joseph Stalin?

During a visit with Joseph Stalin, Winston Churchill attempted to convince the Soviet dictator of the advisability of having the Vatican as an ally. Stalin, the story goes, asked derisively, "How many divisions does the pope have?" When this was related to Pope Pius, he was reported to have commented: "Mr. Stalin will meet my legions in the other world!"

Why was John XXIII's election not cheered by the Vatican tailors?

When Pope John XXIII (Angelo Giuseppe Roncalli) was elected, the Roman tailors who had prepared three sets of white robes (one small, one medium, and one large) had not made any allowance for a man of very large girth, which the former Cardinal Roncalli was. The new pope's first quip as pontiff was: "Everyone wants me to be pope—except the tailors." As he went toward the open window to give his blessing to the masses congregated below, he was heard to mutter something that referred to his constricting clothing with some words to the effect about "the shackles of the papacy."

Which pope had a reputation for frugality?

A penny-wise but pound-foolish administrator, Pius XII diligently watched every dime the Vatican spent. To save on electric current, for instance, he often made the rounds of the papal apartments flicking off the lights. Not infrequently, he refused to make necessary repairs because he didn't want to spend the money. "I cannot," he said, "be extravagant with the funds of the Holy See."

Pius XII also established the Vatican policy of reusing envelopes—intra-Vatican communications were not to be sealed in such a way that the envelope could not be used again. Pius even wrote his last will and testament on the back of an envelope that had already made the rounds.

Which pope considered himself outranked by a soldier?

During World War I, the man who was later to become Pope John XXIII reached the rank of sergeant in the Italian Army's Medical Corps. Shortly after his papal election, when an officer of the Palatine Guard knelt before him, the pope said to the soldier: "Get up! Get up! After all, you are a captain and I was only a sergeant."

How often do bishops meet with the pope?

The Vatican suggests that each bishop come to Rome to see His Holiness personally at least once every five years. He must submit a full, very detailed report on his diocese, and must venerate the tombs of the apostles Peter and Paul during his visit.

Has there ever been a pool-playing pope?

Pope Pius IX (1846–1878)—who actually began his career in the Papal Guard—was a nut about billiards. Having installed two billiard tables (one in the Vatican and the other at Castel Gandolfo), he spent much of his leisure time knocking the balls around the table with a cue stick. Mostly, he played billiards with cardinals or members of the Papal Guard, whom he beat with skilled regularity.

Which pope had a problem learning Latin?

Angelo Roncalli (later to become Pope John XXIII) was not a particularly bright student while in elementary school. More than any other subject, Latin was his stumbling block. As the practice was in those days, priest-teachers did not spare the rod; John XXIII once frankly admitted, "Latin stuck in my head at the rate of about one clout for each word."

Which pope approved the invention of an alphabet?

The inventor of the Cyrillic alphabet was Saint Cyril. This alphabet, for the Church's liturgy and the translation of the Bible, was approved by Pope Adrian II.

Has a layman ever been elected pope?

After several centuries of secret theological discussions (things always move slowly inside the Vatican), the Vatican decided in 1975 to remove a pope from the official papal list, following an encyclical by Pope Paul VI. It seems that one Ottobono Fieschi of Genoa was elected to become Pope Hadrian V in July 1276 (and served about two months before he died unexpectedly). Hadrian V was not a bishop or a cardinal at the time of his election, and, in fact, had never been a priest. In a November 1975 encyclical, Paul VI wrote: "If he who is elected pope has not been ordained bishop, this must be done at once...." With this ruling, the question of Hadrian V came up once again, especially since the Vatican II Conclave had had a discussion over whether a man who was not a bishop could be elected pope. Vatican Radio said that with Paul's ruling, "It would appear that a newly elected pope cannot be considered as the real pope, successor of Peter and Vicar of Christ for the universal Church, as long as he has not been ordained bishop."

Which pope invented a calendar?

The Gregorian calendar, the one used today in most of the world, was issued in 1582. Pope Gregory XIII was annoyed over the Julian calendar, which was devised in 45 B.C. and was 11 days out of kilter. Almost simultaneously, he ordered the establishment of a Vatican astronomy laboratory to study the sun. The observatory was moved out of Rome late this century (away from the glare of the city lights) to the summer residence at Castel Gandolfo.

Photo from Liguori Archives

Monument to Gregory XIII in St. Peter's, Rome.

Which pope reigned the longest?

The longest reigning popes in history were Pope Pius IX (who reigned for 32 years), Pope Leo XIII (who reigned for 25 years), and Pope Pius VI (who reigned for 24 years).

What was the papal attitude toward Hitler?

During World War II, there were two popes, neither of whom favored Adolf Hitler. Both Pope Pius XI and Pope Pius XII did two things that irked the German Chancellor: whenever he came to Rome for a meeting with Mussolini, (1) the pope would always leave the Eternal City for a vacation in his summer home in Castel Gandolfo, and (2) the pope would order the Sistine Chapel closed for repairs. Consequently, Hitler never got the opportunity of seeing the Sistine Chapel, though all his life he yearned to do so.

Which pope undertook the modernization of the Vatican?

Seeking to bring the Vatican up to modern standards, Pope Pius XI (1922–1939) installed the first plumbing, elevators, all-electric kitchen, and a radio station.

Which pope was a hypochondriac?

Pope Pius XII suffered from a number of imaginary illnesses. Among other idiosyncrasies, he had a complex about houseflies, which he bad-mouthed as carriers of diseases. Whenever he sought to swat a fly in his office or bedroom, he chased after it with a fly swatter that he carried at all times on a belt underneath his robe. Among his imaginary illnesses were a chronic toothache of mysterious origin, irregular pulse, and a suspected heart condition, bilious attacks or some other liver disorder, and anemia. Pius did suffer from an inflamed colon and chronic gastritis, but one of his doctors considered even this to be the direct result of his hypochondria.

Pope Pius XII cleaned his teeth many times during the day in a long and complicated ritual—first brushing with toothpaste made especially for him by a chemist, then washing out his mouth with a strong astringent, and finally massaging his gums with sterilized cotton swabs that he dipped in a disinfecting solution. Convinced his gums were bad and listening to none of the advice from competent Vatican doctors, Pius found a Roman dentist who prescribed a "remedy" for the pope's "bad gums," which unfortunately was chromic acid—a strong preparation also used to tan hides. Not only did this cause his gums to become more and more sensitive but also it gradually, over the years, worked on him like a slow poison, causing stomach disorders, spasms of the diaphragm and his well-known attacks of hiccups.

Which Italian pope preferred a German composer to his compatriots?

Though Italian, Pope Pius XII preferred Wagner's operas to those of any other composer. He owned a complete collection of gramophone records and forbade the playing of any of Giacomo Puccini's music inside the Vatican because of Puccini's one-act opera, *Suor Angelica* (Sister Angelica). This particular opera, which Puccini said several times was his own personal favorite, concerned a nun whose family had forced her into the convent after she gave birth to an illegitimate child. On learning of her son's death, Sister Angelica committed suicide by fashioning a poisonous potion she had diluted from plants in her convent garden—as she is dying, the Virgin Mary appeared on stage to grant her full forgiveness and welcome her into heaven where she will be reunited with her lost child. Puccini had based *Suor Angelica* on a true story he heard at the convent where his kid sister was a nun, and where he socialized with the community on his visits. The pope did not approve of Puccini's embellishments of the principal character's story nor of the way he wove the Virgin Mary into the story line, to absolve Sister Angelica of suicide with some of the composer's most heart-wrenching music.

Which pope was responsible for the Vatican irrigation system?

To ensure an adequate water supply for Vatican City and its elaborate gardens and fountains, Pope Pius XI had 9,300 irrigators installed, plus 55 miles of pipelines and 2 reservoirs, each holding 1.5 million gallons of water—coming from Lake Bracciano, outside Rome. At the pope's behest the irrigation system was also equipped with some rather special devices that could mischievously squirt jets of water at an unwary visitor when Pius was in a playful mood. Did the pope love to drench new cardinals when he took them for a walk along the pebbled pathways? You bet!

Was the pope ever headquartered in France?

Contrary to what most people believe today, when the popes lived in Avignon—which served as a refuge for seven pontiffs and as the seat of the "second Vatican" during the fourteenth century—the city belonged to the Kingdom of Naples and was not, strictly speaking, French territory.

Which pope was the son of a farmer?

Pope John XXIII came from a poor family of farmers. The pontiff himself, commenting on his father's poverty, once remarked: "There are three ways a man can ruin himself—women, gambling, and farming. My father chose the most boring way."

Who was responsible for construction of most of the fountains in Rome?

Besides the two fountains in St. Peter's Square, most fountains found today on the streets and squares throughout the City of Rome were built by papal fiat.

One of the many fountains inside Vatican City.

Which pope had the shortest reign?

The shortest pontificate on record is that of Pope Stephen II, who died four days after being elected on March 22, 752. He died on March 25, 752, before his consecration. The succeeding pope took the name Stephen II as well. The ordinal III appears in parentheses after the name of the second Pope Stephen II (III) in order to distinguish the two.

Which pope taught a carpenter how to curse?

The quick wit of Pope John XXIII was once experienced by a French carpenter while Cardinal Roncalli was the nuncio of Paris. As he was putting up a bookshelf, the carpenter hit one of his fingers with a hammer and sputtered a long list of blasphemous words. Roncalli heard these expletives and tiptoed into the room to tell the irate carpenter: "Well, now, what kind of language is that? Can't you say '*merde*' (shit) like everybody else?"

What was John XXIII's famous dinner-party wisecrack?

Known for his sharp wit, Pope John XXIII uttered a wisecrack during his Paris duty as nuncio when a beautiful young woman in a low-cut dress came to a dinner party. Roncalli said to the people around him, "I wonder why when a pretty woman comes in, everyone turns to look at me instead of her to see what sort of face I will make."

Which pope's grave is in Germany?

Pope Clement II is the only pope ever buried in Germany. He died in 1047.

Which pope slept the least?

Pope John XXIII was noted as a person who needed very little sleep. It was not at all unusual for him to retire at 10 P.M., sleep until one in the morning, work throughout the deep stillness of the dark hours until 6 A.M. and then go back to bed for another two hours before beginning his day.

What was Saint Peter's original name?

Saint Peter's real name was Simon Bar-Jona.

Which government has jurisdiction over the pope?

The pope enjoys immunity from the territorial jurisdiction of any human authority. Consider what happened when Hitler's occupation troops in Rome completely surrounded the pope's tiny state. German soldiers never crossed the frontier. Had they, however, decided to invade Vatican City, the blitzkrieg would have taken all of a half hour, and the man who was then pope would have been conquered—but not defeated. In his own way Hitler provided a dramatic confirmation of the real, if intangible, moral authority of the pope, however diminutive his territory. The pontiff's unique position in the world was aptly expressed by one writer who said, "The pope is not sovereign because he is the ruler of the Vatican state; he is the ruler of the Vatican because he is a sovereign."

When and how did Saint Peter die?

Saint Peter's death, in all probability, took place between A.D. 64 and 65, during the persecution of the Christians by the emperor Nero. Nero condemned Peter to be crucified, but feeling unworthy to die in the same way as Christ, Peter requested that he be crucified upside down.

Has a pope ever been assassinated?

Pope John VIII was assassinated in his sleep when an unknown assailant beat him to death with a hammer nine days before Christmas in December 882. As was the necessity for anyone who ruled a city or state in central Italy, Pope John—a soldier by profession—built up his own navy, and in April 876 personally led his naval squadron against Saracen ships, freeing more than 600 captives.

What would happen if a pope were to become mentally enfeebled?

Rome correspondent Robert Neville once asked this question of a Vatican prelate, saying that since popes are elected for life, with no provisions for their recall or for their abdication, what would happen if a pope were to lose his reason? The Vatican officer replied: "The Good Lord seems to protect the Church from such a catastrophe. Popes just apparently do not lose their mind or reason. But should the impossible happen, I believe the Vatican bureaucracy could act as an effective brake against rash or embarrassing acts."

Which pope is known as a soccer fan?

On the day he was to be installed as the supreme pontiff, Pope John Paul II insisted that the ceremony be scheduled at 10 A.M., so as not to interfere with an important soccer match on television.

Which pope was forcibly enthroned?

Pope Leo IV (847–855) was probably the only pope in history who had to be carried to his throne forcibly. As a priest in the Quattro Incoronati Church in Rome, fearful of the hazards of the papal office, he did not want to cope with them at all—and proclaimed his refusal to take on the job of pope. But, once he did so, although against his strong wishes, he built the present-day Leonine Walls of the greatest height and thickness possible, fortified by 44 towers and having only 3 entrances to defend himself against the Church's militant enemies.

Who was the only pope to die violently in an accident?

This was Pope John XXI. While he was asleep, part of a new wing that was being added to the papal palace at Viterbo, Italy, fell on him on the night of May 20, 1277. He had been in office for only nine months.

Which pope was a heavy reader?

Pope Paul VI was the papal bibliophile. On every trip he made abroad, over 75 crates of books were always brought along so that he could take his pick when he retired at night. Paul VI preferred nonfiction to fiction.

Who was Pope Joan?

Officially, the Catholic Church does not accept the existence of Pope Joan. The first mention of her is to be found in chronicles written in the thirteenth century (four centuries after the time that she allegedly reigned). In the fifteenth century the people of Siena erected a statue in her honor in the cathedral. Though many variations to her story abound, the Church maintains that none of these can be documented.

According to the legends, the woman called Pope Joan was either named Agnes or Ghiberta and was born in the city of Mainz, Germany, of English parentage. While still a young girl, she fell in love with an English monk and, disguised in men's clothes, followed him to Athens. Later, she is said to have gone on her own to Rome, where she first took a job with the Church as a scribe, then became a papal notary, was appointed a cardinal, and then made a pope. She ruled, reportedly, for some 30 months.

Which pope got hiccups just before a major broadcast?

One year, just five minutes before he was to begin an Easter discourse in front of a live mike, Pope Pius XII suddenly developed a case of hiccups. With an international radio hookup to millions of people tuned in from everywhere, the pope could not seem to shake off this tricky ailment. As the second-hand of the studio clock raced toward the On-the-Air deadline, staff members tried all kinds of devices to get His Holiness to stop hiccupping. They spun him to the right nine times, covered his head with a paper bag, made him hold his breath, got him to drink some water from the far side of the glass and even tried to scare him with a sudden movement. Someone even tried pounding his back. But nothing worked. A few seconds before the pope went on the air, the hiccups disappeared as mysteriously as they had come. And, yes, Pope Pius XII delivered his words with nary a fluff.

Which pope was a convert?

In the year 498 a convert from paganism (Symmachus of Sardinia) was elected pope and reigned for 15 years. With the zeal of a crusader coming from his new-found faith, the pope built public hostels for the destitute, erected a public lavatory in St. Peter's Square and tripled the level of welfare payments to the poor—with funds coming from the papacy.

Which pope auctioned off his personal automobile?

Pope John Paul II once owned a 1975 Ford Escort. When that automobile went on the auction block—proceeds to benefit a Polish orphanage—the bidding became one of the highlights of the spring 1997 sale at the world's leading collector car auction company, Kruse International. The new owner, who wants to remain anonymous, was the recipient of more than the title to the car. For the $102,000 he shelled out, he received a trip to Rome and a meeting with the pope himself, at which time the pontiff personally handed the keys to the Escort to the proud owner. Included in the package also was a tour of the Vatican and the City of Rome.

Chapter II

Vatican VIPs
and
Visitors

Who is the pope's right-hand man?

Next to the pope himself, the single most important individual in the Vatican hierarchy is his immediate aide—the secretary of state—whose duties correspond to those of the prime minister in other government organizations.

Who was the woman who tried to convert a pope?

Without meaning any insult whatever, Italians like to tell jokes about the papacy. When Clare Boothe Luce was the U.S. ambassador to Italy, one anecdote made the rounds because Mrs. Luce was a convert to Catholicism, and converts, say the Italians, are the most fervent of Catholics. The story is about the time Mrs. Luce was received in private audience by Pope Pius XII. When neither she nor the pope emerged from the chamber for a long time, Vatican aides began to fret. After a few hours they peeked into the room and saw the pope backed into a corner with Mrs. Luce talking a blue streak. Finally getting a word in edgewise, Pius XII was heard to say, "But, Mrs. Luce, I already am a Roman Catholic!"

Why did Michelangelo talk back to the pope?

When Pope Julius II asked Michelangelo, who was at the time in the midst of painting the Sistine Chapel, how much longer it would take before the work was completed, the great artist replied: "Your Blessedness, when it is finished!"

Why was Woodrow Wilson embarrassed when he met the pope?

A personal, official meeting with the pope is very often a mind-boggling experience, even for royalty or a head of state. For instance, when President Woodrow Wilson had an audience with Pope Benedict XV, he took off his top hat and handed it to an usher. But Wilson neglected to take off his overcoat. As he walked toward the pope, a papal chamberlain stopped him at the last second and helped him take off the forgotten coat—much to Wilson's embarrassment.

What cardinal was fluent in 39 languages?

Father Giuseppe Gaspare Mezzofanti, as a parish priest in Bologna, was assigned the difficult job of hearing the final confessions of two Germans sentenced to die in 24 hours—and the young cleric could not understand the language the two men spoke. So that night Mezzofanti set himself down and studied from books on hand the language of the two condemned men—and learned German well enough to preside at the confession and understand fully what the two said.

That started Father Mezzofanti (born in 1774) off on

one of the most peculiar hobbies imaginable: He learned as many languages as he could, studying months upon months without a break. By the time he became Cardinal Mezzofanti and was working in the Vatican, he was sufficiently fluent in 39 languages to carry on in-depth conversations with native speakers.

Cardinal Mezzofanti's languages, in alphabetical order, were Albanian, Algonquin, Amarinna, Arabic, Armenian (ancient), Armenian (modern), Basque, Bohemian, Chaldee, Chinese, Chippewa Indian, Coptic, Danish, Dutch, English, Flemish, French, German, Greek, Guzarati, Hebrew, Hebrew (rabbinical), Hindustani, Illyrian, Italian, Latin, Magyar, Maltese, Persian, Polish, Portuguese, Romanic, Russian, Spanish, Swedish, Syriac, Turkish, and Walachian.

The cardinal—who became known in his day as "the greatest linguist of all time"—also had a good working knowledge of the following languages but did not speak them as fluently as he wished: Angolese, Bulgarian, Chilean, Gaelic, Georgian, Koordish, Mexican, Pegu, Peruvian, Serbian, and Welsh.

And he also understood and could read the following languages—but he would not admit to being able to speak any of them: Aramaic, Bimbarra, Burmese, Cochin-Chinese, Singhalese, Cornish, Frisian, Irish, Icelandic, Japanese, Lappish, Lettish, Oceanian, Malay, Quechua, Sanskrit, Tibetan, and Tonquinese.

In addition, the record shows, Cardinal Mezzofanti had a thorough working knowledge of 37 dialects.

Mezzofanti also maintained that the most difficult language to learn was Basque. Moreover, he firmly believed that his own native language (Italian) was the most beautiful of all languages—and English the most expressive. He was on record as having said that quality Italian (as used by Dante) and quality English (as used by Shakespeare) were unmatchable by any other language.

What language was spoken by Jesus and his disciples?

Besides learning languages, Cardinal Mezzofanti pursued other scholarly instincts, which led him into the historiography of the Aramaic language, the mother tongue of Jesus and his disciples. Mezzofanti delved into Aramaic with intensity because the Old Testament books of Daniel and Ezra were written originally in Aramaic, as was the New Testament Gospel of Saint Matthew. Other portions of the Old Testament (for example, Jeremiah, Esther, Tobias, and Judith) were also written in Aramaic. The cardinal was among the first scholars who addressed himself to the fact that although Pontius Pilate questioned Jesus mostly in Latin, Jesus gave all his replies in Aramaic, through the aid of an interpreter.

Related to Phoenician, Hebrew, Arabic, and Assyro-Babylonian, Aramaic is a Semitic language, and in Jesus' time it was the popular idiom of Palestine. Although Jews of the first century read the Scriptures in Hebrew, they always used Aramaic to converse. Aramaic, which flourished from about 700 B.C. to A.D. 700, was first spoken in Arama (now Syria). Gradually, it replaced

Phoenician and Hebrew in the Middle East, then faded away as Arabic became the popular speech. "Whatever language Jesus used in his time," wrote Mezzofanti, "millions have known the meaning of his words, for He spoke in a voice that went into the hearts of men and will be heard forever by people of all languages."

Note: Aramaic is still heard today in a small Syrian settlement of about a thousand Christians living in the hills outside Damascus. When translated into English, an Aramaic sentence requires many more words. For instance: "Our Father which art in heaven" comes out in two Aramaic words—*Abhinu shebbashamayim.* Written from right to left, the Aramaic alphabet has 22 letters that are basically consonants.

Who are the three uncanonized laywomen memorialized in St. Peter's?

Christina, Clementina, and Matilda are the three "queens" of St. Peter's Basilica. Of the hundreds of statues of popes, saints, and other Church VIPs of the past, three memorials inside the basilica are devoted to uncanonized laywomen.

The Protestant-born Queen Christina of Sweden (1626–1689), who abdicated her throne to become a Catholic in 1654, lived in Rome for 34 years as the number-one celebrity of her time—patroness of composers like Archangelo Corelli and Alessandro Scarlatti and owner of a collection of paintings and books that was the envy of all scholars and intellectuals who sought her company, not excluding many of the popes themselves.

Clementina Maria Sobieski was born in 1702 and belonged to one of the richest and most famous European families (her grandfather was the Polish king who saved Vienna during the Turkish siege in 1683). At age 16 she was to have married James III of England, but on her way to Italy for the wedding, the Austrian emperor (an enemy of James III) had her arrested in Innsbruck, where she was kept a prisoner under the watchful eyes of a company of soldiers. She managed an incredible, almost Hollywood-like escape after a wild five-day chase through the Alps and the Brenner Pass. Her marriage to James was an unhappy one, but there were two sons—one of whom became the cardinal-bishop of Frascati (Italy) and who styled himself Henry IX, "King by the grace of God but not by the will of man." Having spent much of her adulthood close to popes, Clementina died in 1735 at the age of 33.

Countess Matilda Canossa was Italy's Joan of Arc. Born in 1046, she inherited the rule of most of northern Italy at the age of nine. At 18, skilled with spear, battle-ax, sword and lance, she led a cavalry force against an antipope. Her lover was a monk called Hildebrand, later to become Pope Gregory VII in 1073. In time, after Gregory was deposed by a German emperor, Matilda's armies fought for him and for the Church's independence from the emperor. Though she was defeated in one battle after another, she stubbornly kept on fighting until she wore the emperor out. Without a single victory to her credit, the Tuscan contessa had won one of history's most crucial religious wars. The sarcophagus containing her bones gave her the distinction of being the first woman buried in St. Peter's.

Why is the *Pietà* Michelangelo's only signed sculpture?

Michelangelo's famous *Pietà* marble statue of the dead Christ lying on his mother's knees, which graces the first chapel on the right inside St. Peter's Basilica, is the only work he ever signed. The young sculptor, 22 years old at the time, had overheard two travelers one day attributing his supreme masterpiece to a third-rate artist from Lombardy. Angered, he sneaked into the church one night and by candlelight chiseled a message on the diagonal band that crosses Mary's torso: MICHAEL. AN-GELUS. BONAROTUS. FLORENT. FACIEBAT. (Translation: Michelangelo Buonarotti. Florentine. Made This.)

Which U.S. president posed for a Vatican sculpture?

When Jacqueline Kennedy was received by Pope John XXIII in a special audience on March 10, 1962, he told the First Lady something about her husband that she did not know. When the president was 22 years old, it seems he posed for a sculptor who was working on a panel for an altar that is today in the Vatican. Young Kennedy had been spending a week of his summer vacation with friends in England (career diplomat John Wiley and his artist wife, Irene Baruch) while his father, Joseph Kennedy, was Ambassador to the Court of St. James in London. Needing a model for an angel in one of the 12 panels surrounding a life-sized statue of Saint Thérèse of Lisieux, Mrs. Wiley found Jack Kennedy's curly hair and youthful serenity of expression just what she wanted. That panel showed the Kennedy winged angel hovering over Saint Thérèse as she was writing a book, with one hand on her shoulder and the other hand cupping the edge of the volume.

Who was Padre Pio?

Padre Pio, a humble, retiring Capuchin priest, was perhaps the greatest Catholic riddle of this century. The remarkable clergyman (born Francesco Forgione) received his first indication of stigmata in 1915, five years after being ordained. For more than 50 years thereafter, while serving in the monastery of San Giovanni Rotondo on Italy's Adriatic coast, he oozed blood from each of the five spots in which Christ had been wounded. Padre Pio bore the wounds of Christ on his hands, his feet, and the right side of his torso. Because he did not want to become the object of hysterical devotion, he did everything to discourage public adulation, but to no avail. In order to hide his wounds, he wore gloves all the time, except at the 5:00 A.M. Mass, when regulations required his hands to be uncovered. For decades fervent pilgrims and curiosity-seekers flocked to the five o'clock Mass. A number of "proved miracles" were attributed to Padre Pio, although the Vatican hierarchy has not yet endorsed any of these alleged phenomena. Padre Pio received some 5,000 letters a month and drew hundreds of thousands of visitors each year from all parts of the earth. He died in 1968 and is currently a candidate for canonization.

Who designed the front staircase to St. Peter's Basilica?

Unknown to most people who head for St. Peter's Basilica, the staircase that leads up to the doors is based on an idea and a design by Michelangelo. The two statues on either side of the bottom of this staircase were originally to be placed within the Basilica of St. Paul Outside the Walls, which was in the process of being rebuilt. Made in 1838, the statues were, however, by order of Pope Pius IX in 1847, placed at St. Peter's.

How did Michelangelo revenge himself on a papal minion?

In the *Last Judgment*, Michelangelo's masterpiece in the Sistine Chapel, the artist left behind a marvelous inside joke. While in the process of finishing the big painting, Michelangelo was reprimanded by Biagio da Cesena, the papal master of ceremonies, because most of the figures depicted were unclothed. Michelangelo revenged himself by painting da Cesena's own likeness in a corner, showing him not only totally nude but also with the ears of a donkey.

Why didn't Sam Snead get his putter blessed by the pope?

Sam Snead, golfdom's all-time leader in career wins, paid a visit to the Vatican at a time when he was undergoing a shaky interval on the greens. Hoping to have his putter blessed, Snead was bemoaning his troubles to a monsignor while waiting for the papal audience to take place. The monsignor quickly told Snead that *his* putting had become hopeless, too. Whereupon Snead decided not to bother Pope John XXIII about his putter. "I figured," Snead said, "that if a good Catholic living in the Vatican couldn't putt, what chance was there for a Baptist from Virginia?"

What mistake did Michelangelo make in the design of St. Peter's?

When you visit the cupola inside St. Peter's, you will see for yourself the evidence of one of the few times Michelangelo goofed. To see his error, do not take the elevator to the top but trudge up the 145 steps of a spiral staircase. Toward the end of your climb, you will notice some big links of chain. Because Michelangelo had incorrectly estimated the yielding point of the drum, not long after the cupola was finished, cracks began to form in the walls. In order to consolidate the lower edges of the cupola, a gigantic iron chain had to be specially made and affixed. To the end of his days, Michelangelo was mortified by this error.

Photo by Nino Lo Bello

Interior view of St. Peter's Basilica at noontime.

Why did the sculptor Canova get evicted from St. Peter's?

At the tomb of Pope Clement XIII inside St. Peter's Basilica is a statue executed by Antonio Canova. There are two magnificent lions—one sound asleep and the other quite awake—guarding the tomb's entrance. The story about this statue is as follows: On the day the tomb was consecrated, the sculptor (Canova) disguised himself as a beggar and mixed with the public to hear what they were saying about his work. To get him out of the church, Prince Rezzonico gave the "beggar" a few coins and ordered him to go on his way.

Which emperor was refused a papal blessing?

In 1914 Emperor Franz Josef—a conservative autocrat who had already been in power for more than a half century and whose harsh policies against Serbia were among the causes of World War I—traveled to Rome to ask Pope Pius X to bless the Austrian armies. The pope is quoted as having said, "Get out of my sight! Away! We grant a blessing to no one who provokes the world to war."

What U.S. comedian was arrested at the Vatican?

Then there was the American comic Don Novello—who on NBC's *Saturday Night Live* created a personage called

Father Guido Sarducci, a gossip columnist for *L'Osservatore Romano*. He did not amuse the Catholic hierarchy, however, and when he showed up in the Vatican in a priestly black cape, a brimmed hat, pink glasses, and cowboy boots, he did not amuse the Vatican, either. The editor of *L'Osservatore*, outraged, called in the Swiss Guards and had Novello arrested, along with his photographer. Accused of impersonating a priest and taking unauthorized photographs, Novello was detained for nearly seven hours, then was escorted off the grounds by four guards at spearpoint and told in plain Latin he was *persona non grata*. Novello didn't know what *persona non grata* meant—but he got the message.

Who is the Japanese priest at the Vatican?

Father John Bosco Masayuki Shirieda, a Japanese who was at one time a Buddhist and a kamikaze cadet during the Second World War, became a Catholic after learning a lesson from a missionary priest. Upon his return from the war, Shirieda found his home had been totally destroyed by enemy bombs. Caught stealing nails by the missionary priest, the young man was given more nails than he could possibly carry. Later when that same priest lost his life while trying to save the life of one of Shirieda's friends in a fire, Shirieda became a convert and eventually a professor of religion in Tokyo. In Rome, Father Shirieda is today an undersecretary in the Curia.

What were John Paul II's thoughts upon becoming pope?

On Monday, October 16, 1978, the day Cardinal Karol Wojtyla was elected pope, he was led to a small room near the Sistine Chapel (known as the Chapel of Tears), and as he was being robed for the first time as pope in a large silk soutane, he told intimates that he kept thinking over and over again about the novel, *Quo Vadis?* by the Polish writer Henryk Sienkiewicz. Set in ancient Rome during the reign of Emperor Nero, *Quo Vadis?* celebrates the triumph of the persecuted Christians over the cruel regime of Imperial Rome.

How did Giotto become a Vatican artist?

The Vatican discovered Giotto because of a circle he drew. When the pope needed some artwork done in the Vatican, he accepted samples of drawings from many painters—but Giotto merely submitted a circle as his sample. He made the circle by dipping his brush into the paint, and then while keeping his arm tightly against the side of his body, drew a perfect circle by manipulating his wrist. From the sheaf of drawings the artists had submitted, the pope selected Giotto because he became instantly aware of Giotto's amazing talent from the way the circle had been perfectly executed.

Which sculptor created the statue of St. Peter?

This mystery was only cleared up in this century through technical and chemical analyses. These determined that the artist who created the statue was Arnolfo di Cambio of Florence, the same master who created the interior of the cathedral in Florence, and that the statue was made in the year 1300.

Who was the nun who was known for her chic appearance?

Born in Maryland of well-to-do Italian immigrants, Mother Mary Dominic Ramacciotti—a former professor of philosophy at New York University—was the only nun ever given direct permission by a pope (Pius XII) to wear a fur coat, have a permanent wave, use Elizabeth Arden cosmetics, attend receptions given by Elsa Maxwell, go to the opera frequently, and dress with fashionable elegance. She was the founder of Girls' Village in Rome.

What has been accomplished by Vatican astronomers?

Vatican astronomers, whose history goes back to the sixteenth century, have recorded positions of more than 500,000 stars in a ten-volume catalog. One astronomer (Father Pietro Angelo Secchi) invented the meteorograph, which automatically records barometric pressure and temperature at the same time.

Which European queen is buried in the Vatican?

Buried between the floor level of the original St. Peter's Basilica and the present St. Peter's Basilica built above it is the grave of Queen Christina of Sweden (1626–1689). She rests among the tombs of popes which include those of John XXIII, Paul VI, and John Paul I.

Monument of Christina of Sweden whose palace in Rome became a center for art and learning.

Who wrote the Vatican's anthem?

The Vatican hymn was written by French composer Charles Gounod and is played on Vatican Radio at least once a week.

Which secretary of state was summoned for a papal clarification?

One of the most efficient secretaries of state in recent years was the first secretary of Pope John XXIII, Domenico Cardinal Tardini. Though the two men enjoyed an excellent rapport, the cardinal, a stubborn Roman who could not fathom John's desire to "open up" the Church to the outside world, was bothered by his superior's "new ways." Since his office was one floor below the pope's, Tardini had a habit, especially when miffed, of referring to John as "the one up there." Since news tidbits and gossip travel quickly inside the Vatican, it wasn't long before word got to John, who summoned Tardini to his office.

"I'd like to clear up a certain matter," the pope said. "'The one up there' is the Lord, the Eternal Father in Heaven. I'm just 'the one on the top floor.' So, I beg of you, don't throw confusion into the ranks."

Chapter III

Vatican City,
the
Eternal City,
and
Other Papal Places

What constitutes the boundary between the Vatican and Italy?

The border between the State of Vatican City and the republic of Italy is a white line that runs from one end of St. Peter's Square to the other. Most people cross it on their way to the basilica without paying any attention to its political importance. This was the boundary line that Hitler's tanks and troops never dared to cross.

How long does it take to become an expert on the Vatican?

One day as dozens of cardinals, bishops, and assorted clerics surrounded him, Pope Pius XII, in one of his rare good moods, asked two young priests the same question: "How long have you been in the Vatican?" "Three weeks," was the reply. "Aha!" exclaimed the pope. "You are an expert on the Vatican!" When the second priest responded, "Three years," the pope said, "Then you know nothing about the Vatican."

How many rooms are in the papal residence?

The Apostolic Palace, the Vatican City's main building and the one in which John Paul II lives, has more than 1,400 rooms, nearly 1,000 flights of stairs, and 20 court-yards.

What is the loveliest site in Vatican City?

Manicured year-round by a green-thumb staff of 20 workers, the Vatican Woods and Gardens are the most beautiful part of Vatican City—complete with dozens of marble angels, towering trees, shadow-blessed footpaths, flamboyant cannas ranged against green-laurel hedges, and fountains of all shapes, some with lilies afloat in mossy pools. The highlight is the seventeenth-century Galleon Fountain, which has 16 cannons shooting water, as do some of the masts. In the prow is a little boy blowing a

The Galleon Fountain in the Vatican Gardens.

spray through his horn. The Vatican Woods and Gardens are where Mother Nature competes with Michelangelo—and you decide who wins. Bring camera.

How many football fields would fit into St. Peter's Basilica?

St. Peter's Basilica covers nearly 430,000 square feet, enough for a half dozen football fields, making it by far the largest church in Christendom. St. Peter's has nearly 500 columns, over 430 large statues, 40 separate altars, and 10 domes.

How many people visit St. Peter's Basilica in a year?

No other church attracts as many people as the basilica; more than 10 million persons visit every year.

Why do bees adorn the papal altar in St. Peter's Basilica?

Of the millions upon millions of people who have seen the Papal Altar in St. Peter's, either in person or on television (when the pope alone celebrates Mass), few are aware of the very moving human details that Bernini put into his work of art at the behest of Pope Urban VIII during the second quarter of the seventeenth century. The documented story concerns a favorite niece of the pope who experienced a difficult pregnancy. Since it appeared that both mother and child might be lost, Pope Urban vowed that if his niece gave birth to a healthy child and she lived, he would bequeath an altar to the basilica. The baby was delivered safely, and the mother recovered. Commissioned to do the new altar, Bernini—by using the escutcheon of his own family (three bees on a field) as a focal point—told the story of the pregnancy thusly:

The first coat of arms shows the head of the young woman above the field of bees; the three bees represent details of her body, and the ornaments below the field stand for her womb. On the base of the first column is the head of a young and healthy woman with a normal body. On the following coat of arms, Bernini depicted the changes in the pregnant woman and her suffering; her face is distorted with pain, and her body has become quite large. The series ends with a coat of arms no longer crowned with the mother's head—instead there is the head of a baby who is smiling.

Has a baby ever been born in Vatican City?

Though there are women living in the State of Vatican City, no baby has ever been born within the city limits.

How extensive are the Vatican archives?

The Vatican secret archives cover 16 miles of shelves.

How can one visit the Vatican Gardens?

The Vatican Gardens can be visited by tourists in groups of about 30 under the wing of an official guide. You report to the Vatican Tourist Information Office on the left side of St. Peter's Square (adjacent to the public toilet facilities) and join one of the groups that start out in a minibus at 10 A.M. During the height of the tourist season, you are advised to report a day or two in advance and get your tickets ahead of time. Between the first of March and the end of October, there are daily tours except for Wednesdays and Sundays. From the first of November through the end of February, tours are on Tuesdays, Thursdays, and Saturdays.

Landscaping in the Italian style in the Vatican Gardens.

What is the Vatican "helicoptorum"?

What used to be a tennis court inside the Vatican, next to a road flanking the Leonine Wall, is now used as a landing field—which Pope John XXIII once referred to as "our helicoptorum." Both President Dwight D. Eisenhower and President Lyndon B. Johnson used the landing plot when they left Rome after a Vatican visit. Usually overlooked is the fact that beneath the Vatican heliport are two subterranean reservoirs containing about 6,000 cubic meters of drinking water piped in from nearby Lake Bracciano.

Vatican City's helicopter port which was formerly a tennis court.

What is the origin of the Egyptian needle in St. Peter's Square?

The mightiest Egyptian obelisk in the world stands in St. Peter's Square, but until a relatively short time ago, a riddle surrounded the great needle. When it was erected in the center of a Rome arena where gladiators used to fight and charioteers raced, Emperor Caligula (whose reign ended in A.D. 41) had a Latin dedication to his mother (Agrippina) engraved at the base of the obelisk. Then, almost 1,500 years later, Pope Sixtus V ordered the 320-ton monolith lugged from the ancient arena to its present position in St. Peter's Square.

But where did the Egyptian needle come from? It bore no hieroglyphics or words of any kind anywhere, so it remained a mystery—until this century, when Professor Filippo Magi, an archaeologist, began to wonder about the Latin inscription and why it had been carved on an indented rectangle and not directly on the surface of the obelisk. Then he looked more closely as the slanting rays of the sun hit in such a way as to reveal innumerable little holes, about a quarter of an inch deep, scattered among the Latin words. Could they possibly be what remained of holes that once held the teeth of bronze letters of a previous inscription, letters that Caligula ordered removed to make room for Latin words? Could the archaeologist reconstruct the ancient letters just from the positions of the holes? With hundreds of plastic letters made to size, Professor Magi went to work—both guessing and using the principles of cryptography—to solve the puzzle. His detective work paid off. When he broke the riddle and the original inscription could be read, it revealed that the obelisk had been put up in Heliopolis by Caius Cornelius Gallus, a Roman prefect to Egypt who had erected many such monuments to his own glory before he fell into disfavor and committed suicide in 27 B.C.

What are the Raphael Rooms?

After the Sistine Chapel, the greatest art treasure belonging to the Vatican is a series of four rooms on the second floor of the Apostolic Palace known as the Raphael Rooms (or the Raffaello Stanze), for which no sum of money can possibly be cited to give a market approximation of their worth.

As one of the Renaissance's major painters, the man known as Raphael (his given name was Raffaello Sanzio and/or Raffaello Santi) did work in the Vatican after 1508 in the pope's private apartment that marked the beginning of his brilliant career. At papal behest he took over the job from artists who were much better known than himself, and to make room for the "decorations," many works of art had to be erased. Covered over were paintings by such masters as Piero della Francesca, Luca Signorelli, Bartolomeo della Gatta, Lorenzo Lotti, Baldassare Peruzzi, and Raphael's own teacher, Perugino (art lovers, please stop wincing). The four rooms are a miracle, and during the summer months, they are always overcrowded. In the massive painting called *Heliodorus*

Driven Out of the Temple, Raphael added a personal touch: He included his dear friend Marcantonio Raimondi in the painting, as a chair bearer in a German costume. Raphael also put his own face into the painting *School of Athens.* He is to be found behind the figure of Sodoma in white at the extreme far right.

Is the Vatican Post Office profitable?

Annually, the Vatican post office shows a profit—mainly from the sale of special commemorative stamps and the issuing of Vatican coins and medals. Back in the summer of 1981, the Vatican caused a slight postal rhubarb when it issued a commemorative postcard of Pope John Paul II in denominations of 150 lire and 200 lire. Within an hour after the Vatican had opened the sale to dealers and collectors, it had to withdraw the 200-lire card because it was discovered that a picture of the pope was missing an arm, his right one—which he uses to impart the benedictions. The hand had been cleanly severed slightly above the wrist and looked as though it had been canceled out in printing. An investigation of the engraved plate did not reveal any damage at the point where the right hand should have been. Suspicion followed that someone at the Italian State Printing Institute, which does all of the Holy See's postage-stamp and postcard printing, had forged the cards on another printing press and then slipped the defective ones into the full cartons delivered to the Vatican. It is surmised that the forger then held on to large numbers of the postcards to sell later to avid collectors in other parts of the world, while in Rome many people were doing their darndest to track down a card for themselves.

How many Christians were martyred in the Colosseum?

Despite what Hollywood and novelists would have you believe, there is no proof whatever that any Christians died as martyrs on the sands of the Colosseum in Rome. Among Italian historians there is unanimity that the Colosseum was never used to "throw Christians to the lions." Such practices were carried out at the nearby Ro-

Cross in the Colosseum in Rome.

man Circus, a one-minute chariot drive away. In the mistaken belief that Christians died in the 1,900-year-old elliptical structure, Pope Benedict XIV (1740–1758) declared the Colosseum a holy place and ordered a cross erected inside.

It stands today at ground level on the northeast side— and no matter which of the many entrances or arches you use, the big, undecorated wooden fixture (*La Croce del Colosseo*) stands out from the pagan-world walls and draws your immediate attention. But despite the cross's impressive appearance, it constitutes a historical faux pas, and many priests in Rome wonder when the facts are going to catch up.

Pope Benedict's error, however, had its redeeming side. As soon as the cross was erected, the practice of filching masonry stones from the Colosseum to use in constructing other buildings in Rome was halted. The modern world, therefore, owes some kind of debt to Benedict XIV, for he saved the colossal monument from being completely desecrated—even if it was for the wrong reason.

What is notable about the pope's private quarters?

The pope's private apartment has a marble bathroom, several television sets, and a projection room for films.

Where is Rome's most notable keyhole?

One of Rome's least known attractions is a keyhole. Through it you can see three countries at the same time— one of which is the State of Vatican City. The keyhole is to be found on the Aventino Hill in a villa belonging to the Sovereign and Military Order of Malta (S.M.O.M.), which is one of the smallest countries in the world and is located near the Spanish Steps in a parcel of land on the Via Condotti (at Number 68). Closely allied to the Roman Catholic Church and run by papal officers,

View of St. Peter's dome through s.m.o.m. keyhole on Rome's Aventino Hill.

S.M.O.M.—with a population of 80—mints its own money in the form of gold and silver coins and prints postage stamps in the denominations of *grano* and *tari*. In the S.M.O.M. Aventino villa, which is not open to visitors, you can peek through the keyhole of the door to a high-walled garden—and what you immediately see is the entire dome of St. Peter's Basilica perfectly framed in the distance. At the same time, you are looking at three countries—Italy, S.M.O.M., and the State of Vatican City.

What is Rome's "Broken Bridge"?

One of Rome's bridges across the Tiber River—the so-called Broken Bridge—is a kind of left-handed tribute to Michelangelo. In 1550, Pope Julius III asked Michelangelo to fix the span of the bridge, which had collapsed, but when the artist explained that this would require an astronomical sum of money, Julius III turned the job over to another architect who had bragged he could do it cheaper and better than Michelangelo. However, in 1598 the bridge fell into the Tiber a second time, much to the Vatican's chagrin. And that's the way it's been ever since.

Was Vatican City bombed during World War II?

Shrapnel marks numbering more than a dozen can still be seen on one of the walls of the Vatican railroad station as a result of an aerial bombing on the night of November 5, 1943, when four bombs were dumped— the only time Vatican City was hit during World War II. Nobody was hurt, but several windows of nearby Vatican buildings were broken, and a number at St. Peter's shattered. Both the German Luftwaffe and the Allied air forces provided the Vatican with sufficient proof that none of their aircraft was involved. Although the bombs were determined to have been British-made, thereby throwing suspicion on the Allies for a short period, the Vatican

Shrapnel pockmarks on the wall of the Vatican railroad terminal.

Photo by Nino Lo Bello

eventually came up with enough evidence, confirmed by a variety of independent sources, that a fanatic, anti-clerical Fascist, Roberto Farinacci, had organized the raid, largely as a propaganda ruse to embarrass both the British and the Americans.

How many books are in the Vatican Library?

The Vatican Library is not one of the biggest libraries in the world, but it is unrivaled in importance because its shelves and storerooms contain works on the Church that are not available anywhere else. With over a million books, more than 100,000 maps and engravings, and nearly 100,000 manuscripts, the Vatican Library is only open to accredited scholars.

What is the history of the Scala Santa?

The Scala Santa—or Holy Stairs—placed by Pope Sixtus V in the late sixteenth century in a building across the street from the Basilica of St. John Lateran, were brought to Rome by Emperor Constantine's mother (later Saint Helena) in the year A.D. 335. The 28 steps of Tyrian marble (which today are protected by wooden boards) were at one time in the headquarters of Pontius Pilate when he was governor of Jerusalem, and it is believed Jesus went up and down these steps on the day Pilate condemned him to death. The glass-covered bloodstains on some of the steps are allegedly from Christ's wounds. From the very day of installation, the faithful have climbed the steps on their knees; each step requires a special brief prayer. At the top of the Holy Stairs is the ancient Palatine Chapel of Popes (which was the Sistine Chapel of the Middle Ages). On the night of September 20, 1870, when Italian troops were about to march into Rome to end the temporal power of the pontiff, Pope Pius IX was driven to the Holy Stairs, which he ascended, as customary, on his knees. From the top of the stairs, Pius IX sadly blessed his supporters before imprisoning himself inside the Vatican—which he never left again.

The Holy Stairs in Rome.

Why is there a bronze angel atop Castel Sant'Angelo?

There is a story behind the bronze angel brandishing a naked sword atop the Castel Sant'Angelo, originally a circular tomb built in Rome by Emperor Hadrian in A.D. 139 but later used as a fortress. When the city of Rome was hit by a terrible plague in A.D. 590 during the reign of Pope Gregory the Great, he led a procession of prayer to the tomb. As the penitential parade of believers, which had started out at St. Peter's, was on its way back to the Vatican, the pope had a vision: He saw an angel hovering over the tomb, sword in hand. Believing this vision to be God's response to the supplications, the pope declared that the epidemic had indeed come to an end.

Photo by Nino Lo Bello

View of Castel Sant'Angelo Bridge in Rome.

Because no new cases of the plague occurred from the next day on, Pope Gregory the Great ordered the bronze statue erected on the roof of Castel Gandolfo. (Legend and fact are intertwined here because the statue was actually erected in the eighteenth century, but indeed in commemoration of Gregory the Great's vision.)

What security measures have been installed at the Apostolic Palace?

Following the attempted assassination of John Paul II in 1981, the Vatican installed bulletproof glass all along the pope's private terrace atop the Apostolic Palace. The window on the third floor, from which popes often address crowds in St. Peter's Square, now has a bulletproof lectern. These measures provide protection from any sniper positioned with a telescopic rifle either on Janiculum Hill or within a high-rise apartment house outside the pontifical domain.

When did Vatican Radio begin operations?

Tourists in the Vatican Gardens (shown on page 107) make their way toward the first Vatican radio station, which made its initial broadcast in 1931 on equipment by Guglielmo Marconi, inventor of the wireless radio. In fact, it was Marconi's voice that emitted the first words ever broadcast over Vatican Radio when he introduced

Pope Pius XI on February 12, 1931. Using his considerable expertise, Marconi made improvements to Vatican Radio's setup for several years thereafter. Today the main transmitting center is situated 11 miles north of Rome in a compound ten times the size of Vatican City, though one antenna and many of the main offices remain on Vatican grounds. Only once since Marconi inaugurated the station has it gone off the air, and that came about on December 9, 1979, when lightning silenced it for 18 hours.

Vatican Radio Station

How many people can fit inside the dome of St. Peter's?

Sixteen persons can fit comfortably in the bronze globe atop St. Peter's dome.

Are the hooded men who patrol the streets of Rome monks?

The figures you see in robes and sandals wandering around Rome are usually not monks but friars. Cloistered monks stay in monasteries and seldom emerge.

What is the "Bridge of the Four Heads"?

As one of Rome's very oldest bridges, going back over 2,000 years, the Ponte Fabricio leads to the Tiber's only island, the Tiberina, which is largely devoted to providing low-cost hospital care. This particular span is also known by another name—the "Bridge of the Four Heads." Behind that nickname is the true story of Pope Sixtus V (1585–1590) who commissioned four big-name architects to restore the Fabricio Bridge, which had undergone disrepair. During the work, the four men bickered constantly among themselves, and a few times even came to blows. Sixtus kept getting reports of the continuous fighting but waited until the work was done to punish the querulous quartet. The penalty was severe—Sixtus had all four men beheaded on the bridge. Then on the very spot where they lost their heads, Sixtus erected a monument to them—four heads carved out of one block of stone. "Now," he said, "for the rest of eternity, they are committed to a peaceful and quiet unity."

What does the Vatican Historical Museum contain?

Inside the Vatican Historical Museum, built at the behest of Pope Paul VI, are reminders of the papacy's military history. Glass showcases display uniforms of the Papal Artillerymen, the Papal Zouaves, the old Noble Guard, the Guard of Honor, and the Gendarmes. There are also a number of battle mementos from Porta Pia, Mentana, and Castelfidardo, where the pope's army prepared for its last fight. The arsenal of weapons runs a full range from Renaissance cannons and Venetian sabres to 78 Remington muskets. The Papal Navy is commemorated by flags and a model of the Corvette, which carried the name *Immaculate Conception.*

Why is there a church over the site of Nero's grave?

Where the Church of Santa Maria del Popolo stands today at the Piazza del Popolo was once the site of Nero's grave—in fact, the exact spot where the emperor took his life. To mark this point, a huge walnut tree was planted, but people reported to the Vatican that the place was haunted by devils and demons. In 1099, Pope Pascalis II had a vision from the Virgin Mary, who asked him to cut down the tree over Nero's grave, dig up his bones, burn them all together, and throw the ashes into the Tiber River. Doing as commanded, the pope hewed the first stroke of the ax against the tree. In 1472, Pope Sixtus IV erected the Church of Santa Maria del Popolo on the site, and in one of the reliefs in the arch across the high altar, Pope Pascalis is seen cutting down a nut tree.

How many art experts observed the restoration of the Sistine Chapel?

Dr. Fabrizio Mancinelli, director of the Vatican Department of Byzantine, Medieval, and Modern Art and supervisor of the painstaking job of removing more than 400 years of accumulated dirt on the paintings adorning the interior of the Sistine Chapel, said that more than 3,000 art experts climbed the scaffolding to the top after the restorations began in 1980.

"The almost unanimous consensus," declared Dr. Mancinelli, "was that we were discovering a new Michelangelo as we cleaned his works—a different type of painter than we had imagined in the way of color tones and style. As we brought the Michelangelo frescoes back to their original brilliance, we realized that for centuries art scholars and art lovers really knew very little about his work. The discovering of the original chromatic quality of his work in the chapel will provide experts with plenty of material to assess for years to come. Because of the grime which smothered the paintings, the world never clearly recognized Michelangelo's brilliant use of color."

How did blocks of the Colosseum wall become part of Vatican buildings?

Many of the original concrete blocks that were stolen out of the walls of the Colosseum were used to construct buildings today owned by the Vatican, including several structures inside the Vatican.

How long is the Vatican railroad?

The Vatican railroad station serves what is doubtless the shortest railroad in the world, running a mere 2,600 feet, and has no regular train schedule. Mussolini put up the terminal building as a gift; comprising one of Vatican City's curiosities, the candy-colored station (constructed in pink, green, and yellow marble) was described by Pope Pius XI as "the most beautiful station in the world." When the railroad was inaugurated, an apology was made to Pius XI because the tracks hadn't yet been properly connected with the Italian network, and the pontiff was told that this would be done shortly. Replied the pope with a smile, "It seems that you are in a hurry to get rid of me."

John XXIII was the only pontiff to have used the railroad; he and members of his staff made a trip in October 1962 to Loreto and Assisi to offer prayers for the Ecumenical Council. Freight trains arrive regularly, however, with tax-free goods, food, and other necessities, which are stored in the high-ceilinged waiting room. The double-track spur that connects with the tracks of the Italian state railway line enters the pocket-sized domain through a pair of big iron gates that open slowly. Trains are drawn in and out by a small steam locomotive. Under an agreement signed in 1953, the Italian railway system must permit the Vatican the use of the main network and also provide royal coaches for the pontiff. Accordingly, Italy built several "presidential coaches" complete with balconies, kitchen, and sleeping quarters. These are cleaned, polished, and examined daily, ready for instant use, although the Vatican has no regular train schedule.

What are some of Vatican City's vital statistics?

The State of Vatican City
- has fewer citizens than the number of representatives in the U.S. Congress.
- has a zero birth rate.
- has a total of 1,100 people living within its diamond-shaped confines.
- has millions of visitors every year but provides no hotels, restaurants, or entertainment.
- has no traffic lights, public transportation, barber shop,

laundry, newsstand, school, hospital, or garbage collection (as for the last, Vatican City garbage is picked up by a crew from Rome).

- is managed by men of Italian origin.
- has an official language that is dead—namely, Latin.
- has a head of state (the pope) who is not only the country's chief executive but also its entire legislature and judiciary; yet he is neither a dictator nor a despot.
- issues its own postage stamps and coins, but uses Italian money as its legal tender and depends on Italy to transport its air mail. Vatican coins are the same size as Italian coins but have the pope's head engraved on them and usually bear a motto—e.g., "It is better to give than to receive" or "This is the root of all evil."
- has a flag few people would recognize, with two equal stripes of yellow and white with the papal tiara above two crossed keys on the white stripe.
- has its own tiny railroad but no regular train schedule. The double-track spur, entering through a metal gate in the Vatican wall, carries freight trains with supplies.

Citizens of Vatican City

- are not subject to Italian income taxes even though many of them prefer to live in Italy rather than on Vatican grounds.
- who do live on the grounds must get special permission to return after the official 11:30 P.M. closing of the

gates, and an "alien" visitor must leave the country before the frontier shuts down.

- have their quarters assigned to them, are not charged for electricity or telephone service, and pay low rents.
- do most of their grocery shopping on the grounds but go into Rome for everything else. Sources in Rome supply the Vatican with its water and electric power; the Vatican's sanitation system empties into Rome's sewers. Without the help and good will of Italy, the nonself-sufficient Vatican would be unable to function efficiently.

How many people live in Vatican City?

The residents of Vatican City number about 1,100; 95 percent of them are male, and fewer than half have Vatican citizenship. No one is born a Vatican citizen— but all cardinals are automatically citizens even if they live elsewhere. Vatican City does not have a residential sector, as such. Members of the Swiss Guards have their own barracks and apartments. Other citizens live in comparatively new apartment buildings.

How many VIP letters are in the Vatican Archives?

One of the Vatican's most fascinating collections comprises the millions of VIP letters in its archives, a tremendous accumulation from many of history's most important people. Put on permanent display in the Vatican Museum in May 1981 were 236 of these letters. Most notable is a petition from the court of King Henry VIII of England—a parchment two feet by three feet in size—written to Pope Clement VII from 75 signatories who attached 75 ribbons and 75 red wax seals. The king had fallen in love with Anne Boleyn and wanted an heir by her, so he petitioned the pope to let him divorce Catherine of Aragon. As we know, the petition was denied.

Other letters are from Galileo, Copernicus, Erasmus, Napoleon, Voltaire, Rossini, Queen Christina of Sweden, Mary Queen of Scots, Genghis Khan's grandson and heir, and a letter from Pope Paul III to Michelangelo giving him free trips on the ferry across the Po River for life.

Does the Vatican have an intelligence service?

Like any other government, the Vatican employs several people on a full-time basis as part of its intelligence service. One of the Vatican's best secret agents in recent years—a man who never got his name in the papers once—was Walter M. Ciszek, a priest who worked inside the Soviet Union under the name of Vladimir Lipinski. Although he outwitted the KGB for many years, Father Ciszek was eventually found out in Moscow, convicted as a spy for the Vatican, and imprisoned for 23 years.

What is *La Terra di Nessuno*?

There is a piece of land in Vatican City that belongs to nobody—neither to Italy nor to the Vatican. The 1,641 feet of territory snuggled between the two countries is called *La Terra di Nessuno* (No Man's Land) and is one of those geographical curiosities that somehow escapes attention.

No Man's Land can be seen in plain view from afar—it is the Corridoio di Castello (Corridor of the Castel), the corridor built in the thirteenth century by Pope Nicholas III, which stretches from the Castel Sant'Angelo to the Vatican. During the Middle Ages, the narrow link was used by the popes whenever they had to flee for

View of No Man's Land between Italy and Vatican City.

their lives from the Vatican to the circular-shaped Castel Sant'Angelo (the former mausoleum of Emperor Hadrian, which was converted into a fortress).

The covered corridor was used last by Pope Clement VII on May 6, 1527, as the mercenary armies of King Charles V zeroed in on the Vatican and the explosion of cannon was heard on the very steps of Saint Peter's.

Have there been any fires in Vatican City in modern times?

Though the Vatican City-State keeps a 20-man fire department constantly on duty, with a corps of red jeeplike fire trucks, there has not been a single fire at the Vatican in well over a century.

When did the Vatican establish a post office?

The Vatican Post Office dates to the fourteenth century, when a pony-express system carried pontifical messages to all parts of Italy. Located just inside Saint Anne's Gate, the Vatican's main post office handles about 2 million letters a year, more than 6 million postcards, and over 15,000 packages. Generally speaking, its post office is efficient and reliable—and many Romans have come to learn that if they go to the trouble of mailing a letter on Vatican grounds, delivery will be faster and safer.

The Vatican Post Office shows an annual profit, but this comes mainly from the sale of commemorative stamps and issues of Vatican coins and medals. Only once did the Vatican Post Office oversubscribe itself on the printing of a postage stamp. During the 1975 Holy Year, nearly a million unsold Vatican stamps of Pope Paul VI had to be burned.

Where does the Vatican store its white elephants?

The Vatican has a junk shop. In a converted palace called the Floreria are all the things the Vatican does not need anymore but does not want to throw away. In this Vatican "warehouse" can be found portable thrones no longer used; dinner services once used for Vatican banquets; the busts of forgotten cardinals; an array of fans from Persia (they were waved over the pontiff's portable throne before the days of air-conditioning); some badly executed statues of the Virgin Mary; so many carpets that all count has been lost; gilded chairs for dignitaries; coaches adorned with gilded door handles and equipped with a single throne as the backseat; all the abandoned furniture of dead popes—such things as rickety bedside tables, wobbly stools, brass beds (all neatly labeled with the names of their past owners). There is also a collection of bad paintings, many of them gifts to the papacy. Notable among these is one that hung in the Vatican Museum for over 100 years. Presented to Pope Pius IX by Queen Christine of Spain in 1850, The *Mystic Marriage of Saint Catherine* was attributed by art experts to the seventeenth-century Spanish painter Bartolome

Esteban Murillo. When the so-called Murillo masterpiece was found to be a counterfeit, it got stored away in the Floreria.

Is there a dress code for St. Peter's Basilica?

Upon entering St. Peter's, tourists and worshipers are reminded by two conspicuous signs posted in five languages that they must be dressed properly in order to preserve an atmosphere of reverence. Women are not supposed to wear mini-dresses, shorts, or sleeveless garments, and men may not wear walking shorts either. The four ushers in charge of enforcing the Vatican's dress code almost daily get into wrangles with some lightly clad visitors who strenuously object to the rules. One usher, after a fistfight with a German woman's escort, had to be hospitalized.

Then Vatican administrators tried another tack: They decided to station a nun at the door to stem the tide of modern deshabille from swamping the major temple of Roman Catholicism. During the summer of 1972, one Sister Fiorella worked at the job for three months but had to withdraw from the stress of coping with more than 20,000 women wearing garb considered immodest. Then the Vatican came up with still another idea: 800 long black plastic raincoats, acquired from a Milan firm for $2,000, were loaned free of charge to anyone who needed one. But the 800 raincoats disappeared within a week—filched as souvenirs.

Where does the pope live?

The pope and certain official members of the Vatican "family" live in the Apostolic Palace, which is actually a conglomeration of buildings built mostly during the Renaissance. Matched only by the palace of the Dalai Lama in Tibet, the pope's palace is one of the world's biggest. The pope lives in an apartment on the top floor facing St. Peter's Square.

Obelisk in St. Peter's Square. The Pope's apartment is on the top floor, right.

What is considered the coolest spot in Vatican City?

It is the roof of St. Peter's where you find a souvenir shop, a post office, a storehouse for construction materials, and apartments for some staff workers charged with doing constant repairs for the upkeep of the basilica. Atop the roof, as long as you stay in the shade, there is always a guaranteed fresh cooling breeze. This is why young men studying for the priesthood go there as their favorite hideaway to pore over their books.

What types of industry exist at the Vatican?

The making of mosaics is the Vatican's only industry (not counting the issuing of postage stamps). The Mosaic School is responsible for most of the mammoth mosaics found inside St. Peter's. The laboratory, set up in the early part of the eighteenth century, perfected the delicate technique of stone matching and its supply of colored stones, kept in a long corridor lined with nearly 30,000 boxes, is the largest anywhere on earth. Some of the stones, colored by a formula no longer in existence, are over 200 years old; the blue ones and the red ones have yet to be duplicated. There is a showroom next to the workshop where some of the stones can be purchased and shipped to any corner of the globe.

How long does it take to walk around the Vatican?

To walk around the zigzagging walls that surround the State of Vatican City takes exactly 60 minutes.

What is the relics library?

One of the most unusual rooms in the Apostolic Palace is the relics library—a high-ceilinged chamber that is lined from floor to ceiling with steel filing cabinets, shelves, and drawers. With its librarian's ladder standing like a sentinel, the room looks like the inside of a lawyer's library. Under an electric lamp in one corner of the world's most macabre library sits a priest who has one of the most unusual jobs anywhere, a job that very few people ever hear of. His work consists largely of sending tiny boxes and envelopes containing the relics of early saints and martyrs to all parts of the globe. Canon law requires that a relic be enclosed in every altar of every Catholic Church or chapel. Because churches and chapels are inaugurated every month somewhere in the world, the priest-librarian is kept busy filling envelopes with pinches of dust or fragments of bone which are then mailed in registered letters.

What role did the Vatican Information Office play at the end of World War II?

Using its independent status during World War II and its freedom of communication with other countries on both sides, the Vatican handled more than 10 million requests for information about missing persons. With a staff of nearly 900 persons, the Vatican Information Office (organized in September 1939), working over a seven-year period, was able to answer the majority of inquiries regarding the whereabouts of missing families or family members, soldiers, and civilians. The information about missing persons was gathered up by papal nuncios and apostolic delegates and their staffs in every country involved in the war. Having done an efficient job under difficult circumstances, the Vatican Information Office was finally closed down. Though at the time an unheralded success, it has never been given its rightful due. Perhaps the Vatican will one day open up its tucked-away archives on this venture, a noble triumph that few people know about.

How many dogs reside in Vatican City?

A Vatican City law makes it absolutely mandatory that all dogs be registered and kept on a leash at all times. At this writing, Vatican City had only five dogs on the official register.

How good is the telephone system at the Vatican?

The Vatican has one of the world's most efficient telephone systems. In fact, in 1886, it had the world's first central telephone system (invented by Gian Battisti Marzi), a good five years before the United States. On a daily basis, the Vatican receives more than 18,000 calls from the outside; these are fielded by a team of telephone operators from the Six Brothers of the Don Orione Society, who handle a double bank of boards with white buttons. Around Christmastime the number of calls to the Vatican zooms to as high as 25,000 a day.

How much mail does the Vatican get per day?

About 800 pounds of mail—or the equivalent of 25 bags—move into the State of Vatican City every day. Nearly twice as much, however, leaves the Vatican City daily, mostly from tourists sending somebody a letter or card postmarked from one of the four mailboxes of the city-state.

What is the reputation of Vatican Radio?

There is a favorite story that gets told in Rome every now and then about the time that one of the Kremlin aides went into Leonid Brezhnev's office with needle and thread in hand to sew on the top button of Brezhnev's trousers. Totally surprised, the Soviet chief asked how the aide knew about the missing button, to which the aide replied: "I just heard it on Vatican Radio."

All humor aside, the anecdote points out the worldwide reputation Vatican Radio has earned for itself in its more than a half century of operation. Broadcasting in 33 languages (including Esperanto), 225 hours a week to a hundred countries by FM, shortwave and mediumwave, Vatican Radio has a listenership of some 80 million people.

Are there any supermarkets in Vatican City?

Vatican City has one supermarket, but no one may enter or buy anything unless he or she can produce an identification card. Prices are usually lower than in the rest of Rome and Italy, especially on alcohol which carries no customs tax. Half the shoppers in the market are laypeople who live and work in the Vatican, and most of the others are laypeople whose families are historically close to the Church. The remainder of the shoppers are the clerics—who are permitted to nudge their way up the line to the cash register without having to wait their turn.

What was Bernini's ambition for the design of St. Peter's?

Bernini wanted to convey the idea that St. Peter's and Catholicism were embracing any and all who come. His idea was to depict the dome of Michelangelo as St. Peter's head and two semicircles of colonnades as outstretched arms that were gathering the faithful while they moved toward the basilica. Made up of 284 Tuscan pillars and 88 pilasters, the Bernini colonnades took from 1656 to 1667 to be completed. The 140 statues of saints above the columns were carved by Bernini's students, and each one of the works received his personal attention.

The Bernini columns in St. Peter's Square.

Is there a residential area in Vatican City?

Vatican City does not have a residential section as such. There are 50 palaces and office buildings all over the grounds, and many of these provide apartments for the folks who make Vatican City their home.

How many people are employed by the Vatican?

More than 3,000 people work at the Vatican, where no private enterprise is permitted, and virtually nothing is privately owned.

Are there many telephones in the Vatican?

The Vatican has more telephones in proportion to its population than any other nation or city on earth.

What lies under St. Peter's Basilica?

Few people know that under St. Peter's Basilica lies still another church, the Sacred Grottos of the Vatican. In the past this vast underground area was so dark and damp that anyone who visited had to do so with a candle or a flashlight, but during the years of 1935 to 1950, the Grottos were equipped with electric lights and converted into a lower church.

What is unusual about the Vatican Polyglot Press?

The Vatican Polyglot Press is probably the most unusual printing plant anywhere, perhaps the only one of its kind. It can publish a book in Egyptian hieroglyphics or Theban Copt. Boasting more than 40 different kinds of type, the Polyglot can handle scripts like Tibetan, Gaelic, Malgasch, Tamil, and ancient German. The plant has nine different types for Greek, seven for Arabic, four for Hebrew, one for Aramaic (the language that Christ spoke), and two for Armenian and Sanskrit. It also has the only complete set of type for ancient Nestorian Chaldaic.

How can one experience an optical illusion in St. Peter's Square?

Here's a tip about something 99 percent of the people who visit St. Peter's Square overlook completely. There are two black marble disks imbedded in the pavement, both of which are just a few feet from each of the fountains. Position yourself on one disk and cast your eyes on the four rows of Bernini colonnades—hey!—now you only see one row, the front row. The other rows disappear! Step off the disc, and three other rows of columns suddenly are visible, as if by magic. This now-you-see-it/now-you-don't optical illusion is a mark of Bernini's mathematical genius.

What is the most ancient church in Vatican City?

The oldest church in Vatican City is St. Stephen of the Abyssinians Church, founded by monks in the sixth century. Within its very thick walls is the tomb of a monk who died in 1740 at the age of 107. The church was used by Charlemagne who worshiped in its crypt.

What is the Russicum?

Founded by Pope Pius XI for the purpose of carrying Catholicism into Soviet territories, the Russicum was originally started with the idea of training priests of Russian background. But as it became more and more difficult to enroll persons who had emigrated from the Soviet Union, the Russicum opened its doors to non-Russians eager to dedicate themselves to Russian affairs, mainly young priests and seminarists studying for the priesthood. Studies included Russian language, history, literature, and liturgy. All the Russicum students virtually became Russians, thought as Russians, and lived as if in Russia. The library was stocked with books and periodicals in the Cyrillic alphabet.

What happened to graduates of the Russicum during the period of Soviet Communism was not always clear—but from time to time in Rome one heard startling stories of priests being sneaked into the U.S.S.R. (in some cases even being parachuted in), where they carried out their religious mission. What was indeed known was that several Russicum grads, like Father Peter of Bialystok, were burned alive by the Soviet Army during the invasion of Poland. Father Theodor Romza was killed in 1947 in Sub-Carpathian Russia, and another dozen grads were living in Siberian labor camps. One of them was the former rector of the Russicum.

Does the Vatican have a pharmacy?

The apothecary in Vatican City has no sign on it, and is not like American drugstores in that it carries only pharmaceuticals. Nearly 6,000 prescriptions are filled each month by trained pharmacists from Italy, Spain, and Australia.

Located in the same building are the living quarters of the religious brothers who staff the pharmacy and also the outpatient clinic of the Vatican Health Service, which was set up in 1953. Vatican employees and pensioners who participate in the plan, to which they make a monthly contribution from their paychecks, receive free medical and dental care and prescription drugs without charge.

Going back to the year 1277, when Pope Nicholas III named a "pontifical herbologist" to supervise all the pharmacies of Rome and keep an eye on the pope's health, the Vatican pharmacy must be the oldest drugstore in the world. "The pope's drugstore" does not sell greeting cards or candy bars the way American drugstores do, nor does it carry current issues of magazines. But it does sell toothpaste and patent medicines. Notably missing are women's cosmetics and perfumes.

How can Vatican license plates be identified?

Vatican automobiles carry license plates that start with the letters S.C.V.—for *Stato Citta Vaticano* (State of Vatican City). But cynical Romans invariably ascribe another meaning to the initials—*Se Cristo Vedesse!* (If only Christ could see!).

The numbers run from 1 to 142. The pope's private cars are parked in the Apostolic Stable, which was once used for papal horses; all told, there are a half dozen gasoline pumps in the Vatican.

Does Vatican City have street signs?

Since 1973, Vatican City's 30 streets and squares have had street signs. The mailman, however, knows everyone anyway so he doesn't need the signs. When delivering letters to some buildings, he places the mail into a basket that has been lowered from an upper floor on a string and then hauled up.

How many windows are there in the papal residence?

There are 12,523 windows in the Apostolic Palace.

Chapter IV

Everything Else
You Always Wanted
to
Know About
the
Vatican
but
Didn't Know
Whom
to
Ask

How much air traffic occurs over Vatican City?

You won't be annoyed by noisy air traffic when you visit the Vatican. Airplanes are not permitted to fly over the State of Vatican City.

What is the most ornate of the papal treasures?

Among the papal treasures are nine tiaras. The one used for the coronation of Pope Pius X (1903–1914), which is shaped like a beehive and ornately embroidered, is decorated with 529 diamonds, 252 pearls, 32 rubies, 19 emeralds, and 11 sapphires.

Where does the word "Vatican" come from and what does it mean?

The word derives from the Latin *vates,* which means "tellers of the future." This was the name given to a hillside on the west bank of the Tiber River in Rome because daily lineups of fortunetellers used to hawk their "wares" there to passersby on the street. In the fourteenth century, when the papacy was returned to Rome from Avignon (France), the present-day Vatican became the residence of the popes, and the word came to refer to the enclave in the middle of Rome that had become the seat of the Roman Catholic Church.

Does the pope have a private garden?

Although the Papal Gardens, which can be visited by tourists, have been used in the past by various popes of this century, the pontiff has yet another private garden. Located on the roof of the Apostolic Palace, almost directly above the pope's private quarters on the top floor, is a trellised garden of walks, fountains, and shrubs that is cleverly concealed by a false roof so that at no point inside Vatican City can any person observe His Holiness when he is there. Nor can the roof garden be seen with a high-powered telescope from any location in Rome.

What relics are displayed at Vatican festivals?

A Vatican custom that emerges whenever the Church has an important festival is the *ostensio* (display) of three relics from a small chapel in one of the piers supporting the cupola inside St. Peter's. These relics are the Veronica (the veil with which Saint Veronica wiped the face of Christ as he was going to Calvary and on which his features are believed to have been imprinted); a fragment of the True Cross (believed to have been discovered at Jerusalem by Saint Helena); and the point of a lance (believed to be from the one that pierced Jesus' side as he hung on the cross).

Why is one of the bullets that almost killed Paul II in Portugal?

One of the 9mm bullets that seriously wounded Pope John Paul II in the 1981 assassination attempt was placed in a reliquary at the Shrine of Our Lady of Fátima in central Portugal. The pope gave the bullet as a gift because he believed his hospital prayers to Fátima saved his life.

How many meetings were required to effect the 1929 pact between the Vatican and Mussolini?

To make the 1929 Concordat (the treaty between Italy and the Vatican) possible, Vatican lawyer Francesco Pacelli (brother of Pope Pius XII) held his first conversation with an Italian government officer in August 1926. Subsequently, he held 110 conferences with Mussolini's ministers at the Foreign Office, 26 with Mussolini himself, and then sat through 64 lengthy conferences with the cardinal secretary of state, together with 129 private and secret audiences with Pope Pius XI. Finally, he supervised 21 rewritings of the treaty's text before both the pontiff and Mussolini affixed their signatures. The entire matter took 920 days.

Over what did the Vatican go to "war" with another ministate?

In the fall of 1978, the mini-republic of San Marino and the ministate of Vatican City went to "war" against each other. No war correspondents or television crews rushed to the scene, however, because not a single shot was fired—but a few diplomatic salvos were released. It seems the postal authorities of each country were wrangling over which party had the jurisdiction to print the work of the sculptor Pericle Fazzini on a postage stamp.

The art piece in question, which graces the Vatican's general audience hall, was Fazzini's *Resurrection,* and San Marino had made plans to put out a special stamp in its honor. But the Vatican squawked. Threatening serious reprisals, papal watchdogs informed the landlocked republic, plunked in Italy's north near the Adriatic coast, that it had no right whatever to reproduce *Resurrection.*

There followed between the two Tom Thumb countries a series of secret diplomatic discussions—several of which were truly "summit" conferences in that they were held in the castle at the top of Mount Titano, 2,300 feet above sea level. At the conclusion of the productive meetings, San Marino and Vatican City issued a joint communiqué stating that both sovereign nations had agreed that San Marino would substitute the Fazzini stamp with a block of perforated squares commemorating "popular Christmas symbols" instead.

How did a sixteenth-century sailor earn a papal reward?

The great Egyptian obelisk—which is one of Rome's landmarks, although it stands neither in Rome nor in Italy but just about ten yards over the Italian border—is entirely surrounded by the State of Vatican City. Back in 1586, when the obelisk was being drawn into St. Peter's Square by hundreds of horses and thousands of workers struggling with beams, ropes, and scaffolding, the death penalty was ordered for any spectator who uttered even one word. No noise should distract the lifting of the unwieldy 75-foot giant! Soon the friction began to burn the ropes, and it was certain that the obelisk would eventually fall. Suddenly a sailor, aware of what was happening and expert as to what needed to

Obelisk and Pope's fountain in St. Peter's Square.

be done, disobeyed the order of silence at the risk of his life, shouting, "Throw water on the ropes! Throw water on the ropes!" This was immediately done, and the workers finished the job without a mishap. As for the sailor, instead of being executed, he earned a papal reward—the right to supply St. Peter's Basilica with palms on Palm Sunday. His heirs still have the concession today.

Which century had the greatest number of popes?

The most popes ever to be crowned during the course of a single hundred-year stretch was between the years 867 and 965, when a total of 28 popes came into being.

What happens to the thousands of gifts the pope receives from admirers?

Except for art objects, which go into one of the Vatican museums, nearly all the gifts (e.g., camcorders and other equipment) are distributed to families of limited economic means.

What size shoe did Jesus wear?

Christ wore a size 10-³/₄ sandal. You can personally check this unusual item of information if you bring along a tape measure or a ruler. A cast of Christ's footprints is in a small church called Quo Vadis on Rome's Old Appian Way, about an hour's walk from downtown or a short taxi ride away. The story behind the footprint, according to Vatican scholars, is that Saint Peter, on his flight from Rome after having escaped from the Mamertine Prison, met Christ walking on his way into the city and asked Him: "*Domine, quo vadis?*" ("Lord, where are you going?"). The cobblestone that Christ allegedly stood on when he met Peter on the Old Appian Way is the block of stone that bears the footprint. The Quo Vadis Church now stands at the spot of the meeting.

Photo by Jimmy Bedford

Christ's footprints on display in Quo Vadis Church, Rome.

Why isn't Michelangelo's *Moses* displayed in the Vatican?

Because of two "defects" in his statue of Moses, Michelangelo did not want to offer the pope a work he personally had ambivalent feelings about. So the famous *Moses* masterpiece is not to be found today in the Vatican but in the Church of San Pietro in Vincoli, a ten-minute walk from the train station. For one thing Moses' head is too small in relation to the rest of his body, a proportion that Michelangelo did not intend. While the master sculptor was working on the head, he accidentally lopped off

Statue of Michelangelo's Moses.

a large piece of marble and therefore had to fashion the head using the small segment that remained. When he finished the statue, however, Michelangelo was himself overwhelmed by the effect it had on him. So enraptured was he that he began to talk to it. One day he even yelled to it, "Why don't you answer me?" Provoked by the silence emanating from *Moses,* the sculptor struck the statue sharply with his hammer and made a tiny chip in the right knee. Visible today, it is one of the reasons why many curious tourists pay a call on *Moses.*

Who was really the model for the Vatican's statue of Saint Peter?

Inside the Vatican there is a seated statue, said to be a representation of Saint Peter. But the head comes from the thirteenth century, the hands from the fourteenth, and the rest of the figure from the third century. Most Vatican officials believe the statue is a representation of a philosopher whose name is unknown.

What was the *Index Librorum Prohibitorum*?

The Vatican Library also catalogs some 4,000 books that were listed in the Vatican's Index of Forbidden Books (*Index Librorum Prohibitorum*). The Index was created in 1557 by order of Pope Paul IV, whose reign most embodied the Inquisition.

Quite a few of the Index listing of forbidden books forever baffled some Church executives, such as Alexander Dumas's *The Count of Monte Cristo* and *The Three Musketeers*, Oliver Goldsmith's *History of England*, and Edward Gibbons's *Decline and Fall of the Roman Empire*. No reason was ever given for the anonymous bans, so one can only wonder why the Index also included such innocuous documents as a 1664 treatise on the use of unguents for burns, an 1844 Swiss almanac, or a pamphlet on the museums of Italy.

Does Vatican law include the death penalty?

Even though Italy has long since abolished the death penalty, the Vatican still keeps the law on its books—a law that has not been imposed under papal regimes since the 1860s when Rome was under the direct rule of the popes. The last executions carried out under pontifical authority took place during the administration of Pope Pius IX, when two revolutionaries blew up a papal barracks and killed 25 of the pope's troops. The duo, Giuseppe Monti, 33, and Gaetano Tognetti, 25, were beheaded on November 24, 1868. An Italian feature film on the incident, starring one of Italy's best-loved actors, Nino Manfredi, was made some years ago but received no international distribution.

How did a statue of the Madonna foreshadow a tragedy?

To honor Pope Paul VI, whom they admired and respected as a friend, members of the Milan Flying Club staged a rather spectacular ceremonial event in 1975, during the Holy Year. Carrying a replica of the Virgin Mary (which crowns the main spire of Milan's cathedral), several members of the club parachuted into St. Peter's Square in Rome, but as they hit the ground, the statue of Mary cracked. The ill-fated event had an even more disastrous ending! Flying back to Milan in a plane piloted by a World War II ace, the club members were all killed when the plane crashed.

Do non-Catholic countries have diplomatic ties to the Vatican?

Various countries of the world maintain diplomatic relations with the Vatican. Papal ambassadors are to be found not only in Catholic nations but also in Protestant, Islamic, Buddhist, and atheist countries. An ambassador of the pope is called a "nuncio" and has the same status as the ambassador of any great power. If a country does not have a nuncio, the Vatican bypasses the problem by nominating a representative without the official status of an ambassador; such people are called apostolic delegates. In practice that person is given many of the courtesies and privileges extended to ambassadors.

Why are there Christ relics in all of Luchino Visconti's films?

Movie director Luchino Visconti's family had centuries of close ties with the Vatican, and he himself, as a small boy, posed for a painting of the Christ Child, now on public display near Milan. Whenever Visconti was shooting a film, he would include a Christ relic in a scene, mostly to bring him good luck. In one film, for example, he exhibited from the Church of Santa Prassede a section of the pillar to which Christ was bound and whipped (the remainder of the ancient column was brought to Rome in 1222 by Cardinal Giovanni Colonna from Jerusalem), and in another film he showed a fragment from the table of the Last Supper, which is above the tympanum of an altar inside the San Giovanni in Laterano Church in Rome.

Why did the pope remove Saint Nicholas from the official calendar of saints?

Pope Paul VI demoted Saint Nicholas (along with dozens of other saints) by removing him from the Vatican's liturgical calendar of saints. The grounds for Saint Nick's banishment were that there was no proof he really existed.

But in Italy's lower Adriatic coastal city of Bari, where Saint Nicholas is the patron saint and where his bones are reputed to be buried, he is venerated for things having nothing to do with Yuletide. For example, he is the patron and protector of shipwrecked sailors and also the guardian saint of young girls without a dowry. And in Bari, the big day for San Nicola (Italian for Saint Nicholas) is not at Christmastime but in May, on the anniversary of the day in 1087 when sailors came back from Asia Minor with Nicholas's body, and the fourth-century bishop was declared a saint by the Barese people, who built a Romanesque basilica in the old city in his name. To honor Saint Nick's anniversary, Bari's entire flag-decorated fishing fleet takes a symbolic casket out to sea and brings it into port, amid feasting, ceremonies, and street parades.

The Vatican has two grievances against Saint Nicholas: The first is that around the altar where the saint's holy bones were buried is an intricate design on the pavement with some Arabic words that say: "There is no God but God, and Mohammed is his prophet!" Apparently, the Arab artists who were commissioned for the work in the eleventh century imbedded in their design the creed of the Moslem religion, and it was several centuries later that the trick was discovered. When word got out, Bari's local priests did not want to ruin the exquisite floor, nor could they raise the funds to alter it. The Vatican disapproved of their decision to leave the floor alone but offered no money for alterations.

The second grievance is simply that the saint has taken on the role of Santa Claus. The Vatican's weekly newspaper said in an editorial: "He represents a monstrous substitution for the Christ Child and offends the faith," adding that the emphasis on toy-giving is an "insidious form of de-Christianization."

What was the origin of the Swiss Guards?

The Swiss Guards were founded by Pope Julius II, the so-called "Warrior Pope," who as a papal aide was so impressed by Swiss soldiery that in 1478 he got Pope Pius IV to sign an alliance with the Swiss cantons. When he became pope himself, Julius II brought in 150 Swiss soldiers in January 1506, the year the first stone of the new St. Peter's Basilica was laid.

Swiss Guards escort a cardinal in St. Peter's, Rome.

Were the Swiss Guards armed during World War II?

During World War II, Pope Pius XII made the Swiss Guards store away their firearms and patrol the frontier between the State of Vatican City and Italy with just their halberds, pikes, or poignards. This was not the first time a pope "disarmed" his guards (the oldest military corps in existence). They had to lay down their arms on the pope's orders rather than face extermination when Napoleon invaded Rome and carried the pope off to France. (For more on the Swiss Guards, see page 148.)

Which Roman church displays relics of the cross?

One of the relics that draws worshipers is a nail allegedly used to crucify Christ and is to be found in a circular, glass-enclosed silver casket in Rome's Santa Croce in Gerusalemme Church. It is about five inches long and tapers in its last quarter-inch to a blunt tip. There is some evidence to support its authenticity but no positive proof. Several other relics are housed in the same church: three wooden splinters from the cross; a fragment of the tobacco-colored, worm-eaten nameplate placed on top of the cross on Pilate's orders with the Latin inscription *NAZARENUS IUDAEORUM,* and two thorns from the crown placed on the head of Jesus.

What does the name "Jesus" mean?

The meaning of the name "Jesus" is derived from both the Aramaic and Hebrew languages. In Aramaic, Jesus is "Yeshua"; in Hebrew, Jesus is "Joshua." The three words —Jesus, Yeshua, and Joshua—mean savior.

Was Napoleon crowned emperor by the pope?

Pope Pius VII (1800–1823) went to Paris to crown Napoleon emperor in 1804, but when he got there, he discovered that Napoleon had not yet married Josephine in a church ceremony. Before crowning Josephine empress, the pope insisted on a sacramental wedding, which aggravated Napoleon no end. Subtly, Bonaparte got his little revenge, however, by presenting Pius with a triple tiara. One of the gems encrusted in the tiara, a large emerald, had been forcibly extracted from Pius's predecessor (Pope Pius VI) in a military-political maneuver by the French on their march into Italy.

How is the Vatican tailor able to dress the pope so quickly?

As soon as a new pope is elected by the College of Cardinals, he is dressed in robes that fit him on a temporary basis. Since the Vatican tailor does not know the size of the man who will be elected, he makes vestments in three or four sizes—so that when the new pope makes his initial appearance to the masses gathered in St. Peter's Square, he is wearing papal robes that have been hastily fitted to his size and held together only with safety pins, which are not visible.

What Church relic is viewed by millions of people each year?

This is the so-called Throne of Saint Peter, which in 1968 was discovered by scientists to be made from wood dated several centuries after the birth of Christ. (Saint Peter was crucified in Rome either in A.D. 64 or 65.) The ancient throne, encased in bronze, is placed above the Altar of the Cathedral in the apse of St. Peter's. Three other relics by the throne are these: the lance that pierced Christ's side, wood from the True Cross, and the veil used by Veronica to wipe the face of Christ.

What are the opening words of all radio Vatican broadcasts?

Vatican Radio opens its program periods to other countries in the following manner: The opening signal sounds the bells of St. Peter's, followed by the announcement—*"Laudetur Jesus Christus"* ("Praised be Jesus Christ"). This is Vatican Radio.

Why are the feet of Saint Peter's statue so shiny?

The well-known bronze statue of Saint Peter on his throne, sitting upright and dressed in a Roman robe with a key in his left hand and the right hand also raised, has been kissed by many thousands of pilgrims over the last six and a half centuries. One look at the statue and you know that both feet have been the object of the kisses because they are shiny and bright, especially the right foot which is even more worn down than the left one. On important feast days the faithful stand patiently in long lines to touch or kiss the feet in reverence to the apostle.

Throne of Saint Peter, Rome.

Photo by Nino Lo Bello

Why is red the color of the cardinals?

The princes of the Roman Catholic Church are the cardinals, and they are immediately distinguished by the brilliant red of their waist sashes, skull caps, and stockings; they also often wear red cassocks and on special occasions red silken cloaks and a voluminous red train, which is draped over the arms as an ancient Roman would his toga. Red became the cardinal color over 500 years ago, when a Venetian-born pope, Paul II, who loved magnificence and pomp, first put his cardinals into red, a deep red, halfway between scarlet and crimson. At the time, Paul II was himself wearing red all the time. When Pius V was elected pope in 1566, he started a pontifical practice of wearing white as the usual garb. The cardinals have worn red since 1465, and the color has become symbolic of a willingness to shed blood for one's faith.

What church-related entities have diplomatic immunity?

Apart from the State of Vatican City, there are many buildings in Rome that have diplomatic immunity and immunity from all direct or indirect taxes. These include the Holy Office (with its buildings near the Bernini colonnade), the area stretching from those buildings to the Janiculum Hill, the International Institute of the Augustinians, the works of the Fabbrica of St. Peter's, the building housing the General of the Jesuits, and the college and schools of the Propagation of the Faith. Also included are the Romanian and Ruthenian colleges, the offices attached to the basilicas of St. John Lateran, St. Mary Major, and St. Paul Outside the Walls, the Dataria Palace, the old Palace of the Propogation of the Fatih (located at Piazza di Spagna), the Vicariate Palace and the Chancellery, the Academy for Noble Ecclesiastics in Piazza Minerva, the Pontifical Gregorian University, the Pontifical Institute of Archaeology, the Russian College, the basilica and monastery of the Twelve Apostles, and the pope's summer villa at Castel Gandolfo in the Alban Hills.

What is the story behind the Vatican Museum's portrait of Saint Jerome?

One of the most unusual works of art in the Pinacoteca of the Vatican Museum is a rare tempera on wood of Saint Jerome by Leonardo da Vinci. Unfinished, this masterpiece was lost—and then found in two pieces by a cardinal. One piece (the head of Saint Jerome) was being used as a stooltop in a shoemaker's shop, and the other half (the torso) was serving as a lid for a chest in an antique store in Rome.

How did the gift of a pearl to the Vatican lead to three public executions?

In 1438 as a rich Venetian lay dying, he promised that if he recovered, he would make a gift of a pearl to the Vatican from his own private collection. The powerful man did indeed recover, and he did indeed send the promised pearl to Rome—where, to the shock of everyone, it was discovered to have been stolen from a reliquary that was believed to contain the skulls of both Saint Peter and Saint Paul. Intense detective work brought on the arrest of the thieves who, it turned out, had also stolen twelve pearls, three diamonds, two rubies, and a sapphire.

Taken to the Church of Santa Maria in Aracoeli, the thieves were kept on exhibit in iron cages, then dragged through the streets by horses to the Lateran, where their right hands were chopped off—following which they were burned to death. The person who had received these stolen properties and eventually sold them was placed atop a donkey and taken to the Lateran, where he was tortured with branding irons and then hanged.

How does the Vatican celebrate the feast of Saints Peter and Paul?

On the feast day of Saints Peter and Paul, Vatican officials hang a huge floral display resembling a fisherman's net that is suspended between the two tall columns at the main entrance to St. Peter's Basilica.

What is Peter's Pence?

The most lucrative of the Vatican's direct sources of income is Peter's Pence, which averages between $25 million and $35 million each year, derived from contributions made in all parts of the world, wherever there are Roman Catholic churches or dioceses. A custom that developed in Britain over a thousand years ago, when a yearly tax was imposed on householders in favor of the pope, Peter's Pence is now strictly voluntary. The last Sunday in June is usually the day on which the money is collected in Catholic churches everywhere, donated in the name of Saint Peter and Saint Paul. Bishops making their personal visit to the pope carry the money with them in the form of a check, usually for U.S. dollars.

What does *INRI* stand for?

The letters *I, N, R,* and *I,* found on the top of the cross on which Christ died, are a Latin abbreviation that refers to the following words: *(I)esus (N)azarenus (R)ex (I)udaeorum*—Jesus of Nazareth, King of the Jews.

For what purpose did the Vatican hire a private detective?

After a home movie had been secretly made of Pope Pius XII's dying moments and the Vatican discovered that the film was being auctioned off to the highest bidder, officials intervened quietly, hiring a front man to outbid everybody and to buy it outright. Then the Vatican made another unusual move, one guaranteed to make it the laughing stock should it get out—it hired a private detective to find out who had made that movie.

The private investigator, Tom Ponzi, solved the Vatican mystery, zeroing in, after much research, on the pope's private physician, Dr. Riccardo Galeazzi Lisi. Lisi was instantly barred from the Vatican for life and swiftly removed from the rolls of the Rome Medical Association. Immediately thereafter, Lisi left Italy and set up his own rejuvenation clinic in a small town just over the Italian-French border.

How does the Vatican check ancient documents for forgeries?

While digging for a new underground garage under St. Peter's Basilica, workers in 1957 found the grave of an ancient Roman writer who had been buried with his cylindrical copper inkpot, his pens, and waxed tablets. The inkpot still had some ink at the bottom (dried up), and when treated chemically, it was possible to write with the fluid. Using this ink as comparison with the ink used on ancient manuscripts in the Vatican library that were suspect, Vatican experts have been able to determine several forgeries or copies made years later.

How rich is the Vatican?

As one cardinal's aide quipped not long ago, "The Vatican should truly be judged by the companies it keeps." And therein lies a joke that made the rounds some years ago about the late Francis Cardinal Spellman and his business know-how. According to the story, Saint Peter was giving a stately dinner up in heaven and although all the VIP guests had found their places, Cardinal Spellman could not locate his. So he asked Saint Peter. But Peter couldn't find it, either. He looked among the seats reserved for cardinals and then remembered: "Oh, excuse me, Your Eminence, in the seating plan I had you placed with the businessmen." (When Spellman first heard the story, he was greatly amused because he took it as a tribute to his good business sense.)

How large is the Catholic population of the world?

According to the Vatican's semiofficial daily newspaper (*L'Osservatore Romano*), there were, at last count, more than 700 million Catholics in the world, comprising 18.4 percent of the world's population. These people are grouped in 359,000 parishes and 2,456 dioceses.

What is *Opus Dei*?

Opus Dei, which in English means "God's Work" and which was founded in 1928 in Spain by Monsignor Jose Maria Escrivá de Balaguer (who died in 1975), views itself as an educational and charitable movement within the Church. It has more than 70,000 members in over 40 countries. Members get their direction from a manual called *El Camino (The Way)*, a book of 140 pages written by Monsignor Escrivá. Over 3 million copies of this book have been printed with more than 90 editions. In the form of 999 maxims, *El Camino* makes clear Escrivá's opinions on what kind of relationships a human being should have with God. *Opus Dei* followers take these as the ultimate spiritual advice. For the most part the language is direct, firm and authoritarian—as for example:

- "Anything that does not lead you to God is a hindrance. Root it out and throw it far from you."
- "Everything that is done out of Love acquires greatness and beauty."
- "Remain silent, and you will never regret it: speak, and you often will."
- "Have you seen the dead leaves fall in the sad autumn twilight? Thus souls fall each day into eternity. One day the falling leaf will be you."

How many programs does Radio Vatican broadcast?

With a staff of 300 men and women, many of whom are multilingual non-Italians, Radio Vatican sends out nearly 300 programs a week, ranging from papal speeches and blessings to international newscasts and from jazz music to live, direct celebrations of the Eucharist.

How much mail does Radio Vatican receive?

The Vatican radio station receives about 50,000 letters a year from all parts of the world.

What does Radio Vatican broadcast besides programs?

During the early morning hours of each day, the office of the Vatican's secretary of state broadcasts messages—some of them in code—to priests, nuncios, apostolic delegates, and cardinals in all parts of the world. Each Church dignitary knows what time to expect special announcements pertaining to his region. He also receives coded signals from the Vatican to remind him of the "date" he has with his receiver.

In contrast with other stations, Radio Vatican often communicates private messages that will not be understood by anyone but the papal representative for whom they are intended. For instance, one might hear something like this: "Father Tizio, with reference to the information in your letter of the eighth of September, re the peasant woman who sees visions of the Virgin Mary, we have considered your suggestion, but suggest that *ad cantandum vulgas....*"

What is the joke about Cardinal Spellman and Radio Vatican?

Years ago, when NBC correspondent Irving R. Levine visited the station on a press tour and we were told that there was such a daily transmission to the U.S., he asked in jest, "Is that when Cardinal Spellman gets his orders from the Vatican?" The staff spokesperson acting as guide replied with a grin, "No, sir—it's just the other way around."

What would Radio Vatican do in the event of John Paul II's death?

Like every major news organization, Radio Vatican keeps prepared programs and tapes for the eventual death of John Paul II. These are coded by the staff as Day X and would have been used in May 1981 when a Moslem Turkish gunman put three bullets into the Pontiff in St. Peter's Square had the assassination attempt succeeded. The Day X programs consist of a series of broadcasts that can run for several days (in each of 33 languages) and include speeches and statements made in public by the Polish Pontiff. There are also a large number of prepared scripts with adjustable minor alterations for the announcers to fit the events surrounding the pope's demise, funeral, and burial.

Appendixes

Appendix I

More Vaticaniana

There are no rules in book publishing that say trivia items should range in length between short and shorter. In preparing this maxi-tentacled collection of Vatican trivia, I was constantly faced with a dilemma—certain items indeed lent themselves to fuller treatment, not just to a paragraph of four or five lines. I debated what to do about this, and decided an appendix to the book was the solution. Herewith, therefore, is a compendium of scattered subjects that stood in line, impatiently waiting to be given somewhat more space, perhaps even a page or two of explanation. Hence, the need for an appendix to separate the tidbits from the big-bits.

—N.L.B.

1. The Vatican Newspaper

The Vatican's daily newspaper, *L'Osservatore Romano* (founded in 1861) is the world's dullest newspaper, but one of the world's most carefully read publications, circulating in over a hundred countries and wielding an influence well beyond its relatively small circulation of 60,000.

Open in its use of invective when it tackles Communism and totalitarian giants of other political stripes, *L'Osservatore Romano* maintained a feud with Mussolini that lasted throughout the dictator's reign. One issue that really raised Mussolini's hackles was that *L'Osservatore*'s editor, Count Giuseppe Dalla Torre (who ran the paper for more than 40 years until he retired in 1961), steadfastly refused to call Mussolini by his pet title, *Il Duce* (the leader).

The Vatican newspaper does accept some advertising—which comes in through an ad agency that narrowly sifts all potential paid messages and that gives preference to sedate subjects.

A few years ago, however, Johnson's Wax Company placed full-page ads on two different days, showing a large blowup of the front of St. Peter's Basilica with the caption: "Truly Splendid—the Basilica of Saint Peter's Recently Cleaned With Johnson's Wax Products." Although the basilica had indeed been waxed with Johnson's Wax, the Vatican frowned on the ads because they made it look as if the Vatican were sponsoring the product and had accepted free wax, when the truth was that the Vatican had bought and paid for the wax. Johnson's Wax was invited to advertise its products elsewhere.

The Vatican will not allow its daily newspaper to be called an official newspaper, though it is generally considered to be the voice of the Vatican. The Vatican's only official newspaper is the *Acta Apostolicae Sedis*, which comes out four times a year and publishes Church documents, Vatican legislation, and official information in Latin—which makes it the Vatican equivalent of *The Congressional Record*.

Before the *Acta* was published, the Vatican did indeed have an official newspaper called *Diario di Roma*, first printed in February 1829. It had the distinction of being the smallest newspaper ever printed; only one column wide, it measured 2.7 inches by 4.3 inches. The only extant copy of this minitabloid is now in Germany, on display in Aachen's International Newspaper Museum.

2. The Pope's Summer Residence

Visitors who go to Castel Gandolfo—a tranquil oasis some 13 miles from the Eternal City and 1,398 feet above sea level—to see where the popes have been spending their summer vacations since 1626 are usually surprised to find out that the papal residence there is nearly 29 acres larger than Vatican City itself.

Enjoying extraterritoriality, the pope's summer home dominates this tiny town of 3,000 people in the Alban Hills. The residence, which runs almost the full length of the village of Castel Gandolfo, includes three main buildings, a model farm, and an elaborate park.

As might be expected, weekday summer visitors don't get much chance to see the pope, but on Sundays John Paul II does give his blessings at midday, appearing on the residence balcony overlooking the main square. Later, he goes over to another balcony above a courtyard to say the Angelus and to greet the people who gather there (they have special admission passes). In the evenings he sometimes joins groups of young people in sing-alongs that take place in the pontifical gardens.

Most people think the gardens are in back of the palace, but they are actually across the street, hidden behind the religious souvenir shops that flank the square. To get to the gardens, the pope uses a covered elevated walkway from his residence, so he doesn't have to walk on the street.

This terraced park ranks with the most beautiful to be found in all Europe, because it is vigilantly well kept and built atop the ruins of an ancient villa owned by the Roman emperor Domitian (A.D. 81–96).

Not very far away is the papal farm, used mostly to grow fruits and vegetables and to keep livestock. The cows are housed in a blue-tiled stable, and the chickens live in a house and hatchery embellished with mosaics. Close by is an astronomical observatory, which is situated here and not in Vatican City so that the powerful telescopes can be shielded from the city lights of Rome. Although it is possible to visit the gardens, it is a bit complicated in that you must first arm yourself with a letter from any cleric in your home state (or even in Italy) who has reasonably good connections in Catholic circles. Only then can you apply for written permission from the palace director. If you succeed, there's a real treat in store for you on the way to the gardens from the papal home-away-from-home because the walls of the reception room are lined with tapestries and display panels produced by the masters Paolo Veronese and Carlo Dolci.

In the papal apartment in the four-story beige building that dominates the Piazza della Liberta, the pope is served by a permanent estate staff of about 100 men and women who live in adjacent houses on the 137 acres of land that comprise the complex. The pope has a private chapel attached to his apartment, but there is also another one, dedicated to Pope Urban VIII, in which two weddings have been held—one in 1627 for a Barberini prince and the other in 1960, when the daughter of the brother of Pope John XXIII married a mechanic.

For over 360 years the residence has been the main attraction of Castel Gandolfo, itself an unimpressive little town overlooking the dark, volcanic Lake Albano (which served as the site of the Olympic rowing matches in 1960). Having been sent there for his health by a doctor, Urban VIII (1623–1644) took over a dilapidated fourteenth-century ducal castle, and with the help of Gian Lorenzo Bernini and Carlo Maderno (the latter designed the face of St. Peter's Basilica) converted it into a splendid palace. It has been used every summer since, except for 59 years when it remained closed following the overthrow of the Papal States in 1870. Only two popes have died at Castel Gandolfo—Pope Pius XII in 1958 and Pope Paul VI in 1978.

As part of the 1929 Lateran Pacts, Mussolini gave the complex back to the papacy, which then took over the palace, an adjoining villa, and a small family building belonging to the famous Barberini family. These were welded together into what is today the papal summer residence, a rural splendor on a hill. During the Second World War, the palace was used to shelter more than 10,000 refugees from the Nazis, who stood outside in the square with their tanks waiting for Hitler's orders to go in. This order never came.

On any given Sunday when the pope is in residence, between 7,000 and 10,000 people come to the square to see him at noontime. Also during the vacation period, the pope makes a Wednesday appearance around noon for special guests and assorted VIPs, most of whom are from foreign countries in an audience building especially constructed at the edge of town.

Set amid luxuriant shrubbery, the 100-yard-long barrackslike structure is walled with glass and is fully air-conditioned. After entering either on foot or carried by bearers, the pope—clad in crimson brocade—sits on his throne on an elevated platform from where he greets the important guests who—except for those seated in a few rows up front—remain standing. (For these particular meetings with His Holiness, special buses leave at 8 A.M. every Wednesday the pope is on vacation—

departure is from Rome's Santa Susanna Church, Via XX Settembre.)

Buffeted by the refreshing winds of Lake Albano (a welcome relief from Rome's muggy, stifling mid-year weather), cool Castel Gandolfo on Sundays and Wednesdays is nevertheless the summer's hottest tourist target.

3. The Vatican Library

One of the Vatican Library's almost endless jobs is the restoration of old books. This work, with which the Vatican has had many years' experience, is done with methods that are of the Vatican's own invention.

Each book or manuscript has its parchment pages separated and trimmed of ragged edges. Then each page is washed, dried, and pressed, much like a piece of laundry. On any given day one can see manuscript pages hanging across the room from a wire, much like a Monday-morning wash. If there are any holes in a page, new pieces of parchment, matched with microscopic precision, are laminated in such a way that the thickness of the original page is maintained. The restored page is then covered with a sheer, almost invisible silk gauze, which is forthwith fused so that the restored page is stronger than when it was new.

The Vatican's "manuscript hospital" is most proud of the time it restored Coptic manuscripts that had been found buried in the sands of Upper Egypt. It took ten years of solid, steady work to bring the faded sheets back to life.

Since Pope Pius XI was himself a librarian, major innovations were made during his reign, all of which helped to modernize the Vatican Library along American lines. A catalog system with duplicate cards on the model of the Library of Congress in Washington, D.C., a new ventilating system from the U.S. to keep the air from becoming too damp for book bindings, a modern lighting system from New York City, and seven miles of steel shelves from Pennsylvania were all introduced by Pope Pius. He also sent four Vatican librarians to the Library of Congress, the Columbia University Library and the University of Michigan Library to work and study methods used there.

Although the real founder of the Vatican Library was Pope Nicholas V (1447–1455), who ordered that the Vatican's scattered collection of manuscripts be assembled in one place, the probable birth date of the library goes back to Pope Martin V (1417–1431) at the time of the return of the popes from Avignon to Rome. When he brought the Papal Curia back to the Eternal City, Martin also brought the old library and the new purchases the popes had made in Avignon. Many of the manuscripts taken to Rome were, in fact, handwritten copies of books by priests; these were called *scriptores*, a word which the Vatican priest-librarians still use.

4. John Paul II Gives Galileo a Second Chance

On March 12, 1737, when the body of Galileo was being moved from a tiny chamber in the bell tower next to the Chapel of Saints Cosimo and Damiano for final burial in Pisa's Church of Santa Croce, a fanatic admirer of the scientist—a nobleman by the name of Anton Francesco Gori—cut off three fingers from the astronomer's right hand to keep as relics. Two of the fingers are today in the private possession of a doctor and his family, while the right middle finger is in the Museum of the History of Science in Florence. One flight up, in Room Number 6, the withered phalanx is in a showcase enclosed in an egg-shaped, gold-decorated glass container atop a piece of marble, cylindrical in shape, on which a Latin sentence by an astronomer of the University of Pisa has been inscribed. The finger, indeed a curiosity, is pointing skyward toward the heavens and toward heaven in silent, fourth-dimension irony.

In November 1979, in Room Number 6, which is also crammed with many of Galileo's personal possessions (a lens, a compass, two telescopes, thermometers, a chair, and four wooden bed legs), a most significant ceremony was held on the occasion of a most significant event: After three and a half centuries, Galileo Galilei had been exculpated by the Vatican, and Pope John Paul II had made the public proclamation. Galileo had been condemned in 1632 for proving that the earth revolved around the sun, a thesis that went against official Church doctrine and for which Galileo had spent the last nine years of his life under house arrest.

Contrary to popular myth, Galileo never actually dropped unequal weights from Pisa's Leaning Tower to prove or discover certain basic laws in the field of motion. After Vatican condemnation came to him for supporting the heliocentric theories of Nicolaus Copernicus, he publicly recanted, but at his trial issued a famous ad lib: "*E pur si muove!*" ("Nevertheless, it does move!")

While Galileo's case was resting in limbo within the Vatican, Napoleon took the original trial transcript to Paris as part of his Italian booty. After the French monarchy was restored, the dossier was returned to the Vatican in 1846 on condition that it be made available to French scholars at any time they wanted to study it. The Vatican agreed. No French scholars bothered with the documents until the early 1960s, when Father Dominique Dubarle got permission to look at them. An atomic scientist deeply concerned with reconciling the Catholic Church with science, Father Dubarle put together a legal brief, using canon law to defend Galileo, and petitioned the Vatican to reopen the proceedings. However, no pope showed much sympathy for the Dubarle-Galileo cause until the arrival of John Paul II, who has always had a special interest in the scientific work of Copernicus, a fellow Pole who studied at the University of Cracow.

Galileo's relations with the Vatican are complicated, but in essence it is a story of the Church goofing on a grand scale. Based on his observations and calculations with a telescope he had constructed (the best any scientist in the world had so far been able to build), Galilean theory was that the Earth and planets of the solar system revolved around the Sun, and that the Sun—not the Earth—was the center of the known universe. His theory kicked up a fierce controversy within the scientific community of his day. No ivory-tower figure, Galileo wrote his books in a language that everybody could understand; in fact, the Renaissance scientist and mathematician was one of the finest Italian prose writers of the period, and able to put across his ideas at the popular level. Galileo was convinced he had come up with the proof for Copernicus's theory, and he had hoped to devise a natural philosophical system for the people that would center around his conclusions and the Copernican thesis.

How did this eminent scientist become subject to Vatican control? Born in 1564 in Pisa, the same year that William Shakespeare was born and Michelangelo died, Galileo Galilei became a student at Pisa University at the age of 17—and at 19, after several years of working with a pendulum and keeping exhaustive records and charts, he came up with his initial findings about time and motion. By 22 he was on the faculty of the university, but in 1592 he received a good offer from Padua University, from where he was to become known throughout Europe. When he perfected the telescope in 1610, the zealous astronomer became the best-known scientist in the world. He had behind him the grand duke of Tuscany (a member of the power-packed Medici family), who not only contributed generous funds for

Galileo's research but also used his enormous clout to protect Galileo against jealous enemies.

Galileo was a practicing Catholic, and in fact his daughter became a Carmelite nun. Certain that the Church would stand by him, he went ahead and published his developing philosophy. But enemies lurked in wait. Among them were the powerful Florentine Dominican friars, who counterattacked by claiming that Galileo was undermining Holy Scripture; they lodged a formal report on him to the Inquisition (the Holy Office). In 1616, Galileo went to Rome to fight the move to discredit him, but that may have been a big mistake, for the Holy Office did not see it his way and ruled that it was heretical to say that the Sun was at the center of the universe. On the grounds that his publicized ideas were a threat to the public order, the Inquisition admonished him and recommended that he accept the admonition. This meant, under the taint of heresy, he was to keep silence or be punished. Bowing to the pressure, Galileo accepted and withdrew to his villa outside Florence, where be continued to delve further into the science of mechanics, despite a painful case of rheumatism.

As luck would have it, in 1623 a new pope was elected—Pope Urban VIII—who previously was Cardinal Maffeo Barberini. During the Inquisition hearings, Barberini had been the only one to defend Galileo. Now that he sat on St. Peter's Throne, Papa Barberini summoned Galileo down to Rome to pay him a friendly call. For Galileo it was a kind of victory when he visited Urban VIII—then coping with time-consuming major problems posed by the French cardinal Richelieu and the Thirty Years' War. Convinced that the pope and the Vatican would now support his ideas, Galileo went ahead and worked on a new book, the title of which was suggested by Pope Urban himself, *Dialogue on the Great World Systems*. The 500-page treatise won five ecclesiastical approvals before its publication, and the book itself earned popular approval everywhere. Nevertheless, the Holy Office did not see the subject of Copernicus the way Galileo did, and he was summoned to Rome to await trial. What happened to Urban's congenial support is one of those Vatican mysteries that history may never document. Now abandoned by his papal ally, Galileo decided to go it alone.

Although he could have found sanctuary in the Republic of Venice, Galileo—already 70, sick, and infirm—went to the Eternal City to defend his ideas. The Holy Office, which had been percolating a long time over the Florentine's sins, argued that Galileo's new book had violated his promise to keep silent and had advocated Copernicanism. Sustaining two days of rigorous interrogation, much of it under the threat of torture and the fear of being burned at the stake as a heretic, Galileo fell to his knees, recanted his theory, and begged the mercy of the seven who were grilling him mercilessly.

Because of his abject public renunciation, the scholarly giant was not ordered to the stake. Instead he was sentenced to life imprisonment that was commuted on the spot, at Pope Urban's request, to house arrest in Florence (he was also given permission to visit his other home in Siena). Even while under house arrest, Galileo wrote a most poignant letter to the Holy Office in which he pleaded his innocence, adding "…I am in your hands. You may do as you please…."

The Vatican's belated but sincere vindication of Galileo came in May 1983, when nearly 200 scientists, including 33 Nobel laureates and 22 cardinals, attended an audience in the Apostolic Palace's Sala Regia, Pope John Paul II—speaking in French—told the representatives of Science for Peace that the Catholic Church had erred in condemning Galileo 350 years ago. He said that the Church's seventeenth-century scientific position came from culturally influenced readings of the Bible. He added: "We cast our minds back to an age when there had developed between science and faith grave incomprehension, the result of misunderstandings or errors which only humble and patient re-examination succeeded in gradually dispelling….I would like to say that the Church's experience, during the Galileo affair and after it, has led to a more mature attitude and to a more accurate grasp of the authority proper to her."

The dust has finally settled on the drama, centuries after Galileo's condemnation brought to the fore the issue of intellectual freedom under Roman Catholic authority. But there remains one more final footnote to Galileo's posthumous reconciliation: Perhaps typical of the Curia's way of doing things is that the Vatican's denunciation of Copernican theory was withdrawn as far back as 1835—whereas Galileo's conviction stuck until just recently.

5. Lights! Camera! Action! Vatican!

Perched on the knob of a hill at the fringe of a historically seesaw plain during the early months of 1983, the Yugoslav Croatian capital of Zagreb was abuzz as a film crew, headed by British actor Albert Finney, made preparations to begin shooting a three-hour dramatic special for television on the life of Karol Wojtyla. Entitled, "Pope John Paul II," and scheduled to be shown on Easter Sunday 1984 on the CBS network and then in Australia, Italy, France, Canada, and Brazil, the U.S.-U.K. coproduction was eventually to be sold as videotapes in those countries, where many of the world's 700 million Roman Catholics live.

But a few days before the first takes were made, Alvin Cooperman, the film's distinguished producer and the mastermind behind the successful TV series *The Untouchables*, was suddenly informed by the regime's police that he, his cast, and cinematic baggage were being ejected from the country. Permission to shoot the film on location in Zagreb—which had been cosmeticized to look like Cracow after the Second World War—was being withdrawn after several months of preparations. Miffed that already a goodly part of his $4.5 million budget had been spent, but nevertheless undaunted, Cooperman moved his crew across the border into Austria and spread his movie-making team throughout the area of Graz, the capital of Austria's Styria Province.

Ordinarily, when something like this happens to a movie company, plenty of welcome publicity accrues.

Cooperman—wise to the ways of promotion and with a track record that showed a flair for publicity—could have taken advantage of such a natural public relations situation to exploit it to the hilt, but instead he elected to draw a curtain around the expulsion and the film itself. No publicity, no newspapers, no reporters, top secret—those were his orders. Instead of having a paid press agent around, the executive producer told his secretaries to refer any and all inquiries from curious newspersons directly to him.

In Vienna, serving as correspondent for Mutual News and its more than 900 radio stations throughout the United States, Monica Emmer got wind of the expelled movie crew and went to Graz on special assignment from the *International Herald Tribune*, also curious as to why the Yugoslav authorities had expelled the Cooperman production and why everything was all so hush-hush. Things did not go so well for Emmer. She did manage to talk with Cooperman in the lobby of his hotel but found that she would be barred from the set. Not ready to take no for an answer and with no small degree of chutzpa, she got herself out at dawn the next day to the Herberstein Castle, where the shooting had already begun and where she guessed (correctly) that Cooperman would not be arriving until ten o'clock. She had several hours—while Finney was putting on his makeup and the technicians were setting up the equipment and props—to get her story. When Cooperman eventually arrived and found a reporter on the set, he blew his cool and personally escorted her off the premises. The *Herald Tribune* ran her story in May 1983 under the headline, "How Albert Finney Became the Pope."

What exactly had producer Alvin Cooperman been trying to hide? The answer lay in the fact that he was under a kind of obligation to the Vatican, for he had had a private audience with the pope and had been given permission to shoot considerable footage inside the Vatican. In addition, the working script for the film had been approved by two priests from the staff of Cardinal Terence Cooke, then the archbishop of New York. With implicit Vatican approval, the New York Archdiocese had put $1.4 million into the production, while Cooperman obtained the rest of the financing from sources friendly to the Roman Catholic Church on the basis that the project had the pope's personal okay. Which it did. And which didn't cut well, alas, with Yugoslavia's Communist authorities. When they found out that the film was being financed by Catholic money and would inevitably turn out to be a propaganda film for the Roman Catholic Church, the Yugoslavian regime, with no nudge from Moscow, suddenly found the script politically embarrassing. So Cooperman got the boot. But what really mattered to the executive producer was that the Vatican should like the final product, because Cooperman had plans to do an entire series of specials on the papacy, using financing primarily from Catholic Church founts. Because the Vatican did not want it to become common knowledge that the film was under the auspices and guidance of the New York Archdiocese and that the archdiocese was consulting with the Vatican on possible script changes, Cooperman knew what his tack had to be with the press.

The propagandistic value of movies—whether made for television or for general commercial release in theaters—was not being overlooked by the Vatican as the winds of change went whistling through Vatican corridors. Since, in the opinion of the pontifical braintrust, films were the best of all possible promotions, the Vatican began dabbling in the movie business. This activity was not necessarily to make profits at the box office but to disseminate the word of Roman Catholicism wherever it would do the most good—and that would be among the young people of the world who, according to one statistic, went to the movies in the greatest numbers. In short order, the Vatican's new film unit was off to a good start, completing four half-hour productions—one on the pope's visit to Lourdes, one about his meetings with children, one on the pope and the rosary, and the fourth about the assassination attempt on John Paul II in St. Peter's Square in 1981 entitled *The Pardon*. In this last film, the producers did not make any attempt to investigate who was behind the attack but stressed the pope's forgiveness of his Turkish assailant, Ali Agca, and his meeting with the convicted man in Rebbibia Prison.

Vatican bureaucratic eyes were first opened to the magic propaganda possibilities of films when a Hollywood company made a movie *The Shoes of the Fisherman* in 1968. In this film Anthony Quinn played the part of a Russian elected as pope. His "election" had to be filmed inside a cardboard Sistine Chapel because the Hollywood producer drew a blank when he formally requested permission from the pope's office to shoot the scene on the actual premises, even though a substantial sum was offered. If past experiences were any criteria, Church officers always kept their reserve about actors and movie cameras within their territorial domain, yet everyone in the Curia was eminently pleased with the positive effect of the film. A box-office success that earned general plaudits, as Quinn played the part of a fictitious but lovable pope, *Fisherman* had enhanced the image of the Church for a broad audience.

In still another film, *The Cardinal*, produced and directed by Otto Preminger in 1963 (based more or less on the life of Cardinal Spellman), the Vatican—having condemned the film on all kinds of grounds and having sought at the outset to stop its production (even including publication as a novel)—was quite surprised at the favorable reaction it got from devout Roman Catholics all over the globe.

Coming as no surprise, it took a long time before the Vatican finally made up its mind about giving its benediction to the silver screen. In 1977 the Italian state television, R.A.I., produced a colossal film, *Jesus of Nazareth*, that Franco Zeffirelli directed as a five-part series. After the first installment had been seen by an estimated 22 million viewers, the Vatican's semiofficial daily, *L'Osservatore Romano*, gave it wholehearted approval and pronounced it "capable of translating in images the sublime dimension of faith." On the other hand, the Italian Communist

Party press called for an investigation into the "scandalous amount of federal funds that were spent to air *Jesus of Nazareth*, an operation of such low artistic-cultural merit and of such pressing clerical importance."

The lessons the clergy learned from these films (and several others of lesser renown) were enough to prompt Vatican officials during the autumn of 1983 to set up their own film unit. The unit's mandate was not only to explore possible movie properties that would project an image of the Vatican corresponding to its own idea of itself but also to put them into production with papal financing. Necessarily, in keeping with the usual Vatican policy of the past, all of this was to be kept, as much as possible, a secret. The film unit was to have a low profile and the Vatican downplayed its existence.

After films came television. In the summer of 1984, Pope John Paul II appointed Archbishop John P. Foley of Philadelphia to head the board of directors of the Vatican's new television production center, which is officially known by its Latin name, *Centrum Televisificum Vaticanum*. The Church has created the TV center with an eye toward making it a full-fledged television station that would broadcast on a daily basis. To start off with, the center began producing and distributing religious television programming that included documentaries of the pope's foreign trips.

Vatican TV and film activities were not without precedent. As early as 1945, the legendary Italian film director Vittorio De Sica was asked by Pope Pius XII to make a commercial movie with Vatican money.

Yet in November 1974 when De Sica died at age 73, none of the obituaries or eulogies made mention of this Vatican-produced film, which was never shown to the public at all. The motion picture was financed entirely by papal money, but when Church officials evaluated De Sica's finished product, the black-and-white movie was never released for distribution.

Bearing the Italian film archive register #562, De Sica's film—which took nearly two years to make and cost the Vatican less than $40,000 to produce—was titled *The Gates of Heaven* (*La Porta del Cielo*). The script, by Cesare Zavattini, has a strong religious theme along lines suggested by Pope Pius. The Vatican never gave any reason, either publicly or privately to De Sica himself, as to why the first movie it had ever produced was "squashed."

This virtually broke De Sica's heart, because he not only considered it a masterpiece of cinematic neo-realism, on a par with his *Bicycle Thief, Shoe Shine*, and *Two Women*; he was also convinced it was the finest film he had ever made. He remained of this opinion all his life.

This is also borne out by his son, Christian, who owns the only extant copy of *The Gates of Heaven* outside of the Vatican itself. However, in his apartment in downtown Rome, Christian gave me a private showing of a 16mm print of *The Gates of Heaven*. For obvious legal reasons, the copy Christian De Sica has cannot be shown in any theater, nor is he prepared, for the time being, to reveal how he came by it.

Lasting an hour and 25 minutes, the film deals with

several people on a train from Rome to Loreto who seek a miracle at the famed sanctuary of "The House of Mary," brought to Italy from Nazareth in the year 1294. The movie shows one old woman traveling to Loreto to pray that the ever-quarreling members of the family she has served as a governess for many years will find peace. On the same train is a young laborer, recently blinded in a factory mishap (shown in flashbacks), accompanied by a coworker who is tormented by the fact that he was directly responsible for the accident. The cast also includes a young pianist who does not believe in God; yet he is on his way to Loreto to seek a miracle that will bring back the use of his hand, which has become paralyzed. In the same car are two young orphans—a girl and a boy. They meet a semiparalytic businessman who takes a liking to the two children and decides to bring them into his home and support them. How each of the train's passengers finds his own miracle, even before the train reaches Loreto, is the main thrust of the film.

"My father often spoke of this film at home," Christian explained on the occasion of showing it to me. "He saw the finished, edited version only once in his life, but my mother has viewed it several times and agrees that it was his best movie ever. She is of the opinion that if *The Gates of Heaven* were ever to be released, despite its now being over fifty years old, it most certainly would receive a nomination for an Oscar as one of the best foreign films of the year."

Ironically, the man the Vatican placed in charge of

the production—and who was, in effect, De Sica's boss on the set—was a young cleric by the name of Father Giovanni Montini, who 18 years later, in 1963, was to become Pope Paul VI. De Sica used to tell an anecdote about Padre Montini: When the young priest visited the set for the first time, he asked if he could look through De Sica's camera. Italian filmmakers have a custom that whenever an outsider looks through a camera for the first time, he has to buy drinks or coffee for everyone in the crew. A good sport, and at great expense to himself though he was then as poor as a church mouse (no pun intended), Father Montini took the company to the Rome train station bar, fished into his purse and found enough coins to pick up the tab, including a beer for the amused American soldier assigned to keep a watch on the set.

Years later, after Montini had become pope, De Sica had reservations about inquiring of him privately as to the fate of *The Gates of Heaven*, because by then he was a nonpracticing Catholic and had violated Church teaching by marrying Maria Mercader while still legally wed to another woman. Defying the Vatican's and Italy's then no-divorce laws, he became, legally, a French citizen though still living in Rome, and then married in France where he had obtained a divorce. A meeting with the pope thus became *verboten*. Mercader, De Sica's third wife and mother of Christian De Sica, was a costar in *The Gates of Heaven*, together with Massimo Giroti and Marina Berti.

"Papa," adds Christian, "used to make a kind of wisecrack about *Gates*. Several times I heard him say: 'To get that film into the theaters, it probably will take God—and a miracle!'"

And who knows? This miracle may have a chance of becoming a reality if the Vatican powers-that-be give De Sica's film a second look and realize that they have a winner on their hands.

6. The Making of a Saint

Altogether, more than 2,500 saints have "marched in" in the nearly 2,000 years of Roman Catholic history—and before the new century comes parading by, perhaps a few more saints will step into the heavenly ranks. "Perhaps...."

That's an important word in the making of saints, for it's not easy to become one. For instance, Joan of Arc had to wait almost five centuries, Saint Albertus Magnus waited seven centuries, and one VIP by the name of Christopher Columbus is still waiting. So, too, is Pope John XXIII, the beloved pontiff who graced the Throne of Peter in the Vatican from 1958 to 1963. Ditto for his predecessor, Pope Pius XII, who died in 1958 after reigning for nearly 20 years. The list of proposed saints is quite long, and at this writing there are some 1,500 candidates who are currently being considered. Since the mid-seventeenth century, the Church has admitted only about 250 saints, compared with the very large number before that period.

All in all, the path that leads to sainthood is a long

and complicated procedure that can cost hundreds of thousands of dollars. What could take a century or more to complete—as the *causa* (proposition) for sainthood sluggishly creeps through the intricate mechanism of the Vatican's meticulous, painstaking procedure—can for brevity's sake be put thus:

A prosecutor, popularly known as the "devil's advocate," is appointed to attack all evidence, and the opponent is called "God's advocate." The process of beatification (by which a person is deemed "Blessed") precedes canonization (becoming a saint), and the procedures for both beatification and canonization are more or less the same (details later). Before a beatification, however, there is the step of veneration, at which time a candidate becomes venerable.

The laborious process of making a saint takes place in an adjunct office of the Vatican's Sacred Congregation for the Causes of Saints. Dubbed more familiarly by Vatican people (lay and clerical alike) as the "Factory of Saints," this adjunct office is housed on the fourth floor of a building facing St. Peter's Basilica. The door leading to the sparsely furnished room is unmarked; its walls are crowded with shelf after shelf containing thousands of oversized scarlet binders that hold the dossiers of the "halo aspirants." On almost any day of the week, inside the little room are a priest and his four busy assistants, also clerics, who undertake the rather fearsome job of examining the backgrounds of the applicants for sainthood and sifting the evidence.

This team has the job of scrutinizing all the facts with

radar eyes to make sure that everything is checked according to canon law. Primarily, this office seeks to coordinate and systematize the search for the truth, a fact that means an application invariably has to be sent back with recommendations for more examination and further clarification in order that the *causa* for a saint be made crystal clear.

During the early years of the Church, saints were canonized quite easily—on the basis, very often, of an individual's having achieved local renown for holiness.

The Church looked upon these "saints by popular acclaim" as having made it, inasmuch as "the voice of the people is the voice of God." Such relaxed methods produced a large number of saints (obscure to us today). It wasn't until the year 993, during the reign of Pope John XV, that the Church saw its first formal papal canonization—that of Saint Ulrich of Augsburg, Germany. In the latter part of the twelfth century, Pope Alexander III formally reserved to the papacy the right to authorize veneration of the dead, but not until 1634 did this rule become practice. Once the Sacred Congregation for saint-making was set up to oversee the complicated process, the procedures that are in force today began.

In the cases of John XXIII and Pius XII, they were first nominated by Pope Paul VI, so the Vatican itself appointed a postulator, or agent, to gather evidence of the two candidates' credentials. The Church is never in a hurry to put anyone's name on the roster of saints—for instance, Joan of Arc, burned at the stake in 1431, was only canonized in 1920. The modern speed record, by the way, is held by Mother Cabrini; she died in Chicago in 1917 and was canonized in 1946, the first U.S. citizen to receive sainthood.

In the normal course of things, the canonization process for a candidate begins when the people of a given locale or members of a religious order in any part of the world decide that the departed one should be made a saint because he/she was during that lifetime indeed a saint. Not every saintly person ends up as a saint, however.

Whenever a candidate for sainthood is put up for consideration, the burdensome task begins with the compilation of evidence of said candidate's heroic sanctity, holy life, saintly disposition, and the miracles attributed to him or her. This is the primary step toward veneration and is taken by a person or a group technically known as the petitioner (the backers of a potential saint), who must pay the immense costs from beginning to end. (The Vatican never makes any kind of outlay of funds on this score.)

Initially, the petitioner (a person or a group) approaches the local bishop with a formal request. Said bishop then inquires of the petitioner about the candidate's reputation for sanctity, the mode of death, and the miracles performed during or after death. Forthwith, the question of public worship comes up, which requires the petitioner to go to the applicant's grave, deathbed, birthplace, and any other sites where the person in question may have had a profound experience. Finally, all this evidence is freighted off by the bishop to the Vatican with an official letter indicating his endorsement. Rome now directs the petitioner (also sometimes called the postulator) to assemble a first brief, and he, with an assistant, must go about getting additional known facts about the candidate; this would include every letter, sermon, speech, article, essay, or book that the aspirant may have written—especially including important remarks that may have been made during the course of his or her life. All this is collated and shipped to Rome, where at least two theologians will examine each word microscopically, with an eye to meeting the standards of religious orthodoxy. The dossiers for each contender are stuffed with millions of words of written and printed evidence assembled by dedicated postulators, historians, clerical detectives, researchers, and secretaries to get the person's name to the first stage—veneration.

The promoter of the faith (the so-called "devil's advocate") now has the unpopular job of picking apart the evidence, seeking out mistakes in fact, errors of interpretation, documentation omissions, and procedural flaws. Some people think of this as red tape, but if the candidate is in any way to be discredited, that is when it would happen—for the job of this office is to establish whether the nominee has a strong enough case for introducing the *causa* to the Vatican powers-that-be.

By this time evidence has been gathered on the candidate's theological virtues—faith, hope, charity, prudence, temperance, justice, and fortitude. The would-be saint must absolutely have all of these in the heroic degree—that is to say, beyond mere goodness. Once convinced of this, the examining office turns the application over to the pope, who at this point can decide on rejection. If, however, the pontiff agrees, he issues a decree of heroic virtue and the step of veneration has been achieved. The person in question from now on can be called venerable.

At last the candidate's case can be considered as officially introduced, following which the Sacred Congregation will appoint five judges to sit in apostolic process to conduct a full-scale investigation of the formal process under way. This is a fact-finding search for even more detailed evidence involving the candidate's sanctity, miracles, martyrdom, and the circumstances of his or her death. When this evidence is ready, the supplicant—who by now is officially referred to as the "Servant of God"—must wait another 50 years for consideration for beatification by the Sacred Congregation. (Sometimes this half-century delay is waived.)

Now a research commission is set up under the supervision of the same local bishop. With it emerges the sticky matter of miracles. These are defined as God's proof of a candidate's heroism and do not include ecstatic trances or apparitions of the Virgin Mary. A miracle, in the Vatican's eyes, is an event that God produces outside the laws of natural order. For beatification, when there are no eyewitnesses to miracles, then the candidate needs three miracles; if the candidate has eyewitnesses, then two miracles are needed. Quite a few saints have needed three miracles because of circumstances that have to do with the value and the type of the miracle.

On the subject of miracles, it must be stated that what was considered a miracle in, say, the sixteenth century may not necessarily be considered a miracle in the twentieth century. This makes sense, considering modern science and its progress and discoveries about natural phenomena. Thus the Church now has stiffer criteria for miracles. The most likely miracle that will be accepted by the Church today falls into the area of a divine cure of a serious illness (such as leukemia, polio, or cancer) for which there is no medical explanation. Medical cures attributed to intercession by a candidate are examined by a panel of nine doctors from Italy, seven of whom must be specialists in the disease or condition under scrutiny, and all of whom must agree unanimously that the cure is miraculous and not medical or biological. So tough has such a criterion become that one high-ranking Vatican official recently told this writer that "even some of our Lord's miracles might not get by today."

In spite of this seemingly impossible medical barrier, when the canonizing of Philadelphia's bishop, John Nepomucene Neumann (1811–1880) came about in June 1977, the nine Roman physicians gave Neumann a unanimous vote on the medical miracles wrought after his death. The miracles approved for beatification were submitted to every possible sort of test to prove their validity; they were cures in 1923 for acute peritonitis and in 1949 for a skull fracture and other severe injuries sustained in an automobile accident. Pope Paul VI declared Neumann as "Blessed" in 1963 because these two cures were unexplained by natural reasons.

What finally qualified Neumann for the final step of canonization (sainthood)—after 91 years of examinations—was the cure attributed to him in the case of a six-year-old boy in 1963, stricken with Ewing's sarcoma, a usually lethal form of bone cancer. In each of these cases, the memory of Neumann had been invoked. The costs of Neumann's case came close to $1 million. He was the third American—but the first American male—to achieve sainthood. He was preceded by naturalized American Frances Xavier Cabrini and American-born Catholic convert Ann Bayley Seton.

After the miracles, virtues, and claims to martyrdom have been ascertained, the candidate is now close to beatification (not yet a saint, of course). There follows a rather complicated set of requirements. A picture must be painted of the candidate, now known as "Blessed"—an image of his or her entry into heaven to be hung above the *sedia gestatoria*. Other paintings of the candidate's miracles will be hung from the piers of the basilica's great dome. In addition, there are booklets and holy cards of the blessed printed, usually into the high thousands. Whatever relics of the blessed can be acquired—such as his or her hair, bones, skin, and garments—are put into reliquaries. A portrait of the blessed must be presented to the pope, who also gets a relic from the corpse, a bouquet of artificial flowers (not fresh flowers), and a published biography that is bound especially for the pontiff.

There is also a two-hour morning ceremony in St. Peter's (which has to be rented at a cost of $10,000), and then there is another ceremony of 30 minutes in the afternoon. At the precise moment of the climax of all the pomp and circumstance, the bells of St. Peter's Basilica ring out, and a triple "Amen" is sung by the Vatican choir.

The candidate is now beatified. To become a saint, two more miracles (or three, as the case may be) are needed following the beatification ceremony. These miracles will have to be treated with the same intensive examination by the medical doctors as before. This may take 10 years or 100 years or 1,000 years, at which time a decision on canonization is made once and for all.

Note

In 1969 the Vatican cast a critical eye on more than 40 saints and dropped them from the official catalog, or liturgical calendar. Removed were such well-known saints as Saint Christopher (the patron saint of travelers), Saint Barbara, and Saint Valentine. Some of the saints were dropped because doubts had been raised in the last few centuries that they ever existed at all.

Many of the saints removed from the calendar had been the object of hundreds of years of fervent devotion, and they still remain strongly rooted in the emotions of millions of Roman Catholics. The Vatican has explained that the saints who have remained in good standing are important to Catholics all over the world, whereas other saints are optional on the basis of local loyalties. For instance, Saint Patrick is fine in Ireland, but, according to a Vatican official, "holds little interest for the Cambodians."

The action caused problems for many believers, especially in the Latin countries where devotion to saints is particularly intense. Among the saints removed from the list (along with their usually celebrated feast days) were Saint Paul the Hermit (January 15), Saint Maurus (January 15), Saint Prisca (January 18), Saint Martin (January 30), Saint Domitilla (May 12), Saint Boniface of Tarsus (May 14), Saint Venatius (May 18), Saint Pudentiana (May 19), Saints Modestus and Crescentia (June 15), Saints John and Paul (June 26), Saint Alexis (July 17), Saint Symphorosa and her sons (July 18), Saint Margaret of Antioch (July 20), Saint Praxedes (July 21), Saint Christopher (July 25), Saint Susanna (August 11), Saint Eusebius (August 14), Saint Hippolytus (August 22), Saint Sabina (August 29), the Twelve Brothers (September 1), Saints Lucia and Geminianus (September 16), Saint Eustache and his fellow martyrs (September 20), Saint Thecla (September 23), Saints Cyprian and Justina (September 26), Saint Placid and his fellow martyrs (October 5), Saints Tryphus, Bacchus, and Apuleius (October 8), Saint Ursula and her fellow martyrs (October 21), Saints Respicius and Nympha (November 10), Saint Felix of Valois (November 20), Saint Chrysogomus (November 24), Saint Catharine of Alexandria (November 25), Saint Bibiana (December 2), Saint Barbara (December 4), and Saint Anastasia (December 25).

7. The Latin Dictionary (Oh, Those American Words!)

Truly, one of the most unusual moments in the history of Italy's Parliament came some years back when a member of the Chamber of Deputies, debating a current bill to suppress the instruction of Latin in Italian high schools, delivered a speech that lasted a fluent 15 minutes in a language no one present understood: Latin.

It was one of the few times that a deputy of the Christian Democratic Party was not heckled by the Communists, simply because what the speaker had been saying was Greek to them. Unable to criticize something they had found incomprehensible, the Communists decided to issue a formal objection to the use of Latin on the floor of Parliament. A search into the rules and regulations, however, showed that there was nothing in the constitution to support a veto of the use of that ancient tongue in the Chamber. Moreover, further research indicated that the last time Latin had been spoken in Parliament was at the closing session of the Roman Senate, when the Caesars had sung their swan aria.

Up until a short while ago in Italian schools, to the Vatican's great satisfaction, Latin was a compulsory language—and a solid mastery of it was required to enter any of the country's universities. This does not mean that men and women with a college education would be capable of handling conversational Latin—as witness what had transpired in Parliament when the politico delivered his linguistic bombshell.

As to whether Latin is a dead language, the controversy may go on *ad infinitum et ad nauseam,* but when you talk to a Wisconsin-born Carmelite priest in the Latinist section of the Vatican Secretariat of State, one Reginald Foster, he tells you in no uncertain terms (in a modern language) that "Latin is alive, Latin is necessary, and Latin is full of fun. Latin is concise, flexible, harmonious, full of majesty and dignity. And you can quote me verbatim!"

When we met, Father Foster was XLVI (46) years old and offered no objection in the least if called by the Latinized version of his first name, Reginaldus. Reginaldus was in the throes of putting "new life" into the so-called dead language through the new edition of the *Latin Dictionary* published by the Vatican Press. What bugged him most were certain words that had crept into the English language which almost seemed to defy being translated into Latin. But he managed to cope, for he had already conquered such words as television (*imaginum transmissio per electricas undas*), radar (*radioelectricum instrumentum monitorum*), atom bomb (*pryobolus atomicus*), tape recorder (*magnetophonium*), and central heating (*calefacientis aquae ductus*). But help, Help, HELP! he had been having one devil of a time with certain other new expressions, and he had made the Vatican understand why there had to be delay after delay in getting the dictionary finished.

The hardest word to confront was "Watergate."

"Watergate!" roared Father Reginald. "Forget it! No matter how hard any Latin scholar will ever try, that word will never be translated into Latin, or for that matter into any other language. Try defining Watergate, by the way, in a one-word synonym. See! It takes a few sentences before you begin to explain what it means."

"Domino theory?" "On that one I think I'll take a raincheck (*tessera surrogata*)," he moaned.

A newcomer expression into our language, for example, petrodollars, stumped the ecclesiastical lexicographer for a while, but then he came up with a temporary Latin equivalent—*numi americani petrolio comparati.* Unsure whether he would put it into the revised *Latin Dictionary* that way, he wanted to wait until he had had a chance to discuss it with language experts with whom he kept regular contact. Two other words on his not-sure list were *gummi terebrata* (flat tire) and *cellula scansoria* (elevator). Supplementing his regular work in the Vatican, Father Foster served as an editor of *Latinitas,* a Vatican quarterly review written entirely in Latin (circulation: 1,000 copies). Even the ads were in Latin—so that an advertisement for a toothbrush would refer to a *peniculus dentarius* or a half-page display for a safety razor would talk about *novacula ab inferendis vulneribus tuta.*

Having written his Ph.D. thesis on the letters of Cicero—all 827 of them written in Latin—the brown-habited, balding cleric with the boyish exuberance of a motivated scholar worked up a lecture based on 500 of Cicero's most meaningful sentences that display pertinency in today's world.

"The letters are all human," explained Father Reginald, emitting his sparks of infectious fervor, "and they could be used in an introductory course to teach Latin, because unlike most teachers who make Latin a cut-and-dried subject, Cicero's lively way of saying things, especially his frequent use of humor, would keep any student attentive. One thing Cicero was not—he was not a windbag. Windbag in Latin is *loquax*." For the Big Book, as it became known behind Vatican Walls, over 10,000 new Latin words were concocted to supplement the language's original 30,000 words. Because the Vatican thinks in centuries, it had full understanding that time had to be spent on each entry, often as much as three or four months on a single word. Latin is the official language of the Holy See, and the Vatican believes that the new dictionary should be the final word.

One term sponged up a lot of Reginald's time and gave daily headaches—"soul brother." With a very special meaning in the Catholic religion, it also ran into the problem of whether to make it masculine, feminine, or neuter, since "brother" in this context could also refer to a woman.

As an American, Reginaldus—while working with his superiors and the cardinal editor in chief—had a keener ear for stateside neologisms. Americanisms and American slang ate up time before they became part and parcel of the British English spoken in other parts of the world. Father Foster was not uptight (*sollicitatur*) about the newly minted coinage of American English and took a cool attitude (*accettum*) on novel interpretations of old words, euphemisms and the weasel phrases from Madison Avenue, the Pentagon, academia, and so on, which meant that he and the editorial team faced such challenges from terms like "Amtrak," "hard-core," "fuzz," "disco," "stonewall," "freak-out," "gay," "effete snobs," and "male chauvinist pig." Immersed in his realm of the dative, accusative, ablative and vocative cases, not to mention the exacting world of the pluperfect, subjunctive, and the present indicative, the grammarian priests found themselves in choppy waters as to exactly how they wanted to swim.

But Padre Foster and his colleagues had to draw the line somewhere, nevertheless—and these involved words that had been created by journalists and gossip columnists like Liz Smith, who, borrowing their cue from Walter Winchell, sought to draw attention by using cutesy neologisms. Vatican brass refused to translate into Latin such words as "saloonatic," "tripewriter," "schooligans," "chutzpathic," "millionheiress," "blessed event" (that would include "blessed hevent" and "blessed shevent"), "Ameritocracy," "splitsville," "trendency," "apparatchik," and "legislady." Several newcomers that were shunned in the final draft of the Big Book inasmuch as they were particularly obnoxious to Vatican thinking were "wife-swapping," "Playboy bunny," "deep throat," "swinger," and the oft-cited headline, "Hix Nix X Pix," which once appeared in *The Hollywood Reporter*. But, on the other hand, certain journalism gems had not yet been ruled out, and they included the "Big Apple," "Capitol Hill," "chow mein," "Reaganomics," "payola," "Jesus freaks," and "McCarthyism."

Although stymied in a multiplicity of idiomatic frustrations, Reginaldus Foster was convinced that Latin should not maintain the *status quo*, since *ipso facto homo sapiens* would be using the Vatican's *magnum opus* in a world where *tempus* must necessarily *fugit.*

8. Exorcism and the Vatican

A 22-year-old Roman woman, standing just over 5 feet in height and weighing no more than 105 pounds, collapsed one day inside St. Peter's Basilica and began emitting rasping, baritonelike sounds and spouting full sentences and phrases in fluent Latin. After she fell to the church floor and five Swiss Guards had come to her aid, it took all five of them just to lift her limp body, something that ordinarily could have been done by one man alone with just a little show of muscle. Mystified by the phenomenon, each of the soldiers could not understand why a little person of such fragile appearance had become so heavy when it was obvious that the same five husky men could have lifted an automobile with much less effort.

Summoned from his second-floor office in the Apostolic Palace, Monsignor Corrado Balducci talked with "Marcella," as her case history came to be known in the Vatican Archives. But he had to do it in the only language she could communicate in, Latin, which she knew so well that she frequently interrupted the priest to correct his grammatical mistakes. Monsignor Balducci was astonished at how many fine points in Latin grammar she had at her command. But he was to become even more astonished when he learned that Marcella had never studied Latin or, for that matter, even finished elementary school. Rather than place her in the care of a medical doctor, the Vatican had called in Balducci because he was one of the Vatican's two clergymen directly authorized by the Holy Father to perform exorcisms. For, plainly put, Marcella was the victim of a demonic possession, and only an exorcist could give her the help she needed. In the some 25 years he had been a Vatican exorcist, Balducci believed that the case of Marcella was one of his most difficult, because it took him eight months to banish ten demons from her body.

Vatican records described Marcella as sweet, with a light and gentle voice. Yet when she became possessed, the voice would change to guttural and she would speak only in Latin—in spite of the fact that when she was in a normal state, the only language she knew was Italian, the kind of Italian rife with Roman dialect words. During her possessions, as the Swiss Guards had found out, she took on an unexplainable dead weight of more than a thousand pounds. Another incredible aspect to her demonic possessions was her uncanny ability to know what was happening behind her back. Once when Marcella had been taken to St. Peter's, Monsignor Balducci had positioned several priests behind the big pillars, well out of sight and unknown to her, with instructions to read the rituals at the same time. There was no possible way for Marcella to have known about those assisting exorcist priests, yet when they began reading sotto voce, Marcella screamed "No! No!" and ran to each of the clerics behind the columns and, one by one, knocked the holy books from their hands.

At the end of eight months of exorcisms, Monsignor Balducci managed to rid the woman of all her demons except one: She reported that this demon called himself Lucifer and that he had assured her nothing would ever prompt him to leave her body. In desperation, Balducci got Pope Pius XII to make an appearance in her presence, as the exorcist prayers were being intensely recited one day. When he walked into the chamber on tiptoe, as per instructions, she was screaming and struggling at the time. Since her back was turned to him, she could not have seen him come in, yet she suddenly calmed down as if hit by a club. It was at this point that the exorcism of Marcella ended. Today the woman is married, has several children, and leads a peaceful, gentle life. The case of Marcella has been filed away for good.

Another difficult exorcism handled by Balducci was the terrifying case of a 45-year-old nun working in the Vatican; she was found screaming in one of St. Peter's chapels, where she kept vomiting up thick pieces of glass and various kinds of nails. Balducci was assigned by Pope Paul VI (the year was 1977) to handle the exorcism: this episode went into the archives as the Case of the Levitating Nun. A few times while she was on her bed, the bed would move away, and she would remain suspended in midair. After a ten-day exorcism rite, the nun was finally brought back to normal and returned to her duties.

Yet another difficult case, now part of the Vatican's official exorcism file, was that of a 35-year-old man who was possessed by seven demons; each demon claimed to have been inside the man for ten years, tormenting him. Whenever any of these demons spoke, Father Balducci needed four men to restrain his patient, which is not a correct word in this instance, because the man was not medically sick by any means. His demons made him contort his facial features in such a way as to resemble certain animals, which in turn made his mouth imitate the sounds that animal would make, almost to precision. When his face stretched forward like that of a hog, the sound would be the oink-snort of a pig. The man would meow like a cat, or bray like a donkey, and in each case his face would take on the form of the animal. At other times he would squirm on the ground like a snake and hiss. Father Balducci's exorcism lasted approximately 58 hours, at the end of which all seven demons left the man's body at once. The file on this man shows that when he was in a normal state, he could not do any animal imitations, except for the cat; neither could he screw his face successfully to imitate any animal. Moreover, he had no conscious awareness that he had ever done animal imitations to near-perfection.

Still another of Father Balducci's cases, also extremely baffling, involved a Roman bank clerk, aged 23. The young woman showed supernatural powers and knew things that she had no possible way of knowing. She would shout and spit at sacred images, curl up on the ground and swear against the saints. Any time the monsignor made a benediction sign behind her back, which she could not see, she instantly jumped into the air, higher than any human being normally can from a standing position. Once, when Father Balducci approached the girl behind her back with a religious relic nestled in his arms and she did not see or hear him, she again suddenly leaped involuntarily into the air. The exorcism rites took hold on the third day, when the clock struck noon. She screamed with a frightening and terrifying howl, following which she then crumpled to the ground as if dead. "That howl was the departure of the devil," the woman's case history stated.

The Vatican's exorcism catalog of well-documented cases contains the details of a 14-year-old boy in Washington, D.C., on which William Peter Blatty based his bestselling book, *The Exorcist.* The case, which was handled by a Jesuit priest from St. Louis University, was not a pure instance of demonic possession but rather a simple case of poltergeist phenomena. But the priest stayed with the boy constantly for two and a half months, during which time the Jesuit went on what is known in Catholic doctrine as "the black fast" (water, bread, and prayer) and lost 50 pounds. In May 1949, the ancient ritual brought on the hoped-for result. Similarly, as with other cases in the Vatican files, the boy during his possessions spoke rapid Latin, a language he had never studied and of which he knew nothing when in his normal state. The Jesuit priest's name must necessarily remain in the archives, largely because he had not obtained permission either from the Vatican or his archbishop to employ the solemn ritual. Nevertheless, he made a full report to Rome on the more than 30 "performances" that were used to bring the young man permanently away from the evil spirit. The Vatican is of the belief that the well-intentioned Jesuit, who was totally inexperienced, had bungled the job because he did it strictly on his own and did not petition for professional help from Rome.

Just in case an exorcism rite is not exactly clear in the reader's mind at this point, let it be said that both Monsignor Balducci and Father Ventura explain it as a rite that is essentially a command from God for an evil one to depart the body of a human being who has become possessed by this evil one (the Devil, in most cases). The exorcism rites, as practiced by the Catholic Church today, were issued in 1614 by Pope Paul V in a document designed to formalize practices that had emerged since the early days of Christianity. Over the centuries this rite has retained its basic features, placing special emphasis on the identification of diabolical possession, selection of the exorcist, and the outlining of the texts (and the setting) to be used during the rituals.

As outlined in the revised Rite of Exorcism (issued in 1999), the exorcism rites cover 84 pages and begin with a series of prayers, psalm readings, and an initial command to the unclean spirit, whoever he might be. Gospel passages concerning possession are read; the stole of the priest and his right hand are placed on the possessed individual, and—interspersed with the sign of the cross—made on the person's forehead and chest, specific words of exorcism are spoken. Here is the text of one such passage:

> I adjure thee, thou old serpent, by the judge of the quick and the dead, by thy maker and the maker of the world, by him who has power to send thee to hell, that thou depart quickly from this servant of God *[name of the possessed person]*, who returns to the bosom of the Church, with fear and the affliction of thy terror. I adjure thee again, not in my own infirmity, but by the virtue of the Holy Ghost, that thou depart from this servant of God *[name]*, whom Almighty God hath made in his own image. Yield, therefore; yield, not to me but to the Ministry of Christ. For his power compels thee, He who subjugated thee to his cross. Tremble at his arm, He who led the souls to light after lamentations of hell had been subdued. May the body of man be a terror to thee, let the image of God be terrible to thee. Resist not, neither delay to flee this man *[woman]*, since it has pleased Christ to dwell in his *[her]* body. And although thou knowest me to be a sinner, do not think me contemptible. For it is God who commands thee. The majesty of Christ commands thee. God the Father commands thee. God the Son commands thee. God the Holy Ghost commands thee. The sacred cross commands thee.

The faith of the holy apostles Peter and Paul, and of all other saints, commands thee.

The Rite of Exorcism advises an exorcist to add a variety of prayers like the Our Father, the Hail Mary, and the Apostles' Creed, which should be repeated as often as possible for as long as the struggle permits. Since Latin is the language most often spewed out by a possessed person, the exorcist should use Latin at all times on the theory that the evil spirit understands this language, since this is the language the victim is forced to speak against his or her own will or knowledge thereof.

Vatican exorcism experts, both in the past and today, have not yet worked out a definitive theory as to how exactly a person can get taken over by a demonic force. In the Vatican's view, a possession is an internal seizure of one's psychomotor activities and displacement of personality, which makes it appear that another conscious ego (the Devil or an unclean spirit) is present. It is classified as demonic when the entity is distinctly malevolent, with pathologically aggressive or self-destructive tendencies.

Over the past three and a half centuries that the Vatican has been dealing with devil-possession, it has never imposed a fee on a given victim. So far as is known, no exorcism has ever been conducted in front of an audience or an outside spectator. Even the pope is not allowed to watch. Several other rules and regulations were broken by the priest in the movie, *The Exorcist*, but the

Vatican does not condemn the film even though it kicked up a hullabaloo; it made known to a wide public for the first time that God as a power is strong enough to overcome the Devil's influence. Even though the movie was factually inaccurate, the Vatican owns its own copy, which it uses as a teaching device. One of the first things the new Polish pope did was to see the movie two times in one sitting.

9. The Pope's American Souvenir

Pope John Paul II has a souvenir of his American travels. No stranger to U.S. soil, which he once visited as the relatively unknown Cardinal Karol Wojtyla of Cracow, he acquired a memento of the City of Baltimore—while on a tour of Philadelphia in 1976—which today hangs in a frame in his office apartment overlooking St. Peter's Square.

The rectangular frame, almost magazine size, contains a simulated piece of parchment with some quaint, homespun philosophy entitled simply, "Desiderata," attributed—erroneously—to the Old Saint Paul's Church in Baltimore, dated 1692. ("Desiderata" was actually the work of an American poet, Max Ehrmann, who published it in 1927.)

At first blush, the document—bearing all the appearances of the kind of kitsch often sold to tourists visiting abroad—appears to be a takeoff on the Ten Commandments, minus the biblical prose style. It strikes one as something that could be called "Eight Rules That Can Help You Be a Better Human Being Throughout Life."

Himself a scholar and philosopher of considerable intellectual powers, the likes of which his world admirers appreciate, the first Polish pope in history was struck by the down-to-earth philosophy of the "Desiderata" message. He bought it, framed it, and had it hung up in his pontifical office as a daily reminder of what being a good person is all about.

When the managing editor of *L'Osservatore Romano*, the Vatican semiofficial daily newspaper, peeked at "Desiderata" one day in the pope's office, he inquired as to what the framed message said, since he didn't understand the English. An accomplished linguist, John Paul personally wrote out by hand a translation of the document into Italian for the curious editor, Father Virgilio Levi. "Desiderata" almost immediately became a bestseller inside the Vatican walls. Once it reached the editor-priest's hands, Father Levi made photocopies of the "Desiderata," and within a few days just about everybody in the State of Vatican City had a copy of the unfamiliar American words of advice, which the pope has dubbed with the Latin phrase, *verbum sapienti*.

You, too, can now have your own personal copy, compliments of one editor and one pope:

Desiderata

Go placidly amid the noise & haste, & remember what peace there may be in silence. As far as possible, without surrender, be on good terms with all persons. Speak your truth quietly & clearly; and listen to others, even the dull & ignorant; they too have their story.

Avoid loud & aggressive persons, they are vexations to the spirit. If you compare yourself with others, you may become vain & bitter; for always there will be greater & lesser persons than yourself. Enjoy your achievements as well as your plans.

Keep interested in your own career, however humble; it is a real possession in the changing fortunes of time. Exercise caution in your business affairs; for the world is full of trickery. But let this not blind you to what virtue there is; many persons strive for high ideals; and everywhere life is full of heroism.

Be yourself. Especially, do not feign affection. Neither be cynical about love; for in the face of all aridity & disenchantment it is perennial as the grass.

Take kindly the counsel of the years, gracefully surrendering the things of youth. Nurture strength of spirit to shield you in sudden misfortune. But do not distress yourself with imaginings. Many fears are born of fatigue & loneliness. Beyond a wholesome discipline be gentle with yourself.

You are a child of the universe, no less than the trees & the stars; you have a right to be here. And whether or not it is clear to you, no doubt the universe is unfolding as it should.

Therefore be at peace with God, whatever you conceive Him to be, and whatever your labors & aspirations, in the noisy confusion of life keep peace with your soul.

With all its sham, drudgery & broken dreams, it is still a beautiful world. Be careful. Strive to be happy.

10. "La Popessa"

Shortly after American and British troops had freed Rome, Claretta Petacci—one of Italy's most prominent movie stars, a notorious and much-gossiped-about political figure because she was Benito Mussolini's mistress—paid a call on a nun working inside the Vatican. It was nearly midnight when Claretta, in disguise, was covertly admitted into a reception chamber on the second floor of the Apostolic Palace. Serving as her dictator-boyfriend's representative dispatched on a special mission, the shapely actress met secretly with the most powerful woman in Vatican history, Sister Pasqualina Lehnert, the German-born housekeeper, confidante, adviser, and closest aide to the reigning wartime pontiff, Pius XII.

What Signorina Petacci wanted was for Sister Pasqualina to persuade the pope to help Mussolini escape from the grip of the German Army in northern Italy so that a political solution could be worked out for Italy.

Pasqualina agreed to bring the matter up to Pius, and although the latter at first wanted nothing to do with Mussolini, he listened. Ultimately, the pope agreed to let Pasqualina tell Claretta in a subsequent meeting to advise the dictator to take his plan for peace to the archbishop of Milan. He in turn would relay it to the pope's desk. In time the proposal did reach Pius, and he found nothing to object to in it. Essentially, Mussolini wanted a chance to escape to a neutral country, together with his wife and children and his mistress. Because Il Duce— who was then commanding a large contingent of neofascist fighters collaborating with the Nazi forces up north— had lost all faith in Hitler and was disillusioned with the German plan of conquest, he submitted a proposal whereby he would surrender his troops, thus shortening the fighting period and saving hundreds of lives on both sides. Sister Pasqualina suggested to Pius that the Mussolini offer be delivered to General Dwight D. Eisenhower, supreme commanding general of the Allies. In a handwritten letter to Eisenhower, the pope urged the general to accept the offer. But Eisenhower declined to do so. To get this message back to Mussolini, Pasqualina spent the better part of a day trying to reach Petacci in Mussolini's Milan hiding place, but that was the last contact between the two women, because events moved rather fast. Petacci and her lover were shot and killed near Lake Como after being nabbed by a band of Italian underground freedom fighters.

The extraordinary partnership between Pasqualina and Pope Pius XII lasted 41 years and included all of Pius's pontificate which ran from 1939 to 1958. During this time—a time when the Vatican had to face some of the greatest crises of recent history—this nun was the very closest confidante of the pope. Often referred to behind Vatican walls as "La Popessa," Sister Pasqualina—who was born in August 1894—wielded an unprecedented power in the Vatican—so much so that more often than not, priests and bishops (and sometimes even cardinals) would seek her permission before applying for a papal audience; this was especially so when Pius fell ill for extended periods.

Ironically, there were many people—clergy and laymen alike—who lived in Vatican City and never even met her. Indeed, she was a mystery woman in every sense, though her influence at the highest echelons was such that everybody inside the Vatican talked of her. Most of the clerics who had to deal with Sister Pasqualina did not particularly like her. They considered her, above all, arrogant and bossy; she was known to be short-tempered, blunt, gruff, and despotic. Yet there were others who knew her to be generous, understanding, sympathetic, and extremely wise. A number of cardinals resented her because of her gender; no woman, for nearly 2,000 years, had ever risen to so much authority in a Vatican that had hitherto been ruled fully by men. Moreover, Pasqualina was not one to knuckle to rank, inasmuch as she had the ear of the pope himself.

Sister Pasqualina died at the age of 89 in Vienna in November 1983, after she had taken part in a ceremony commemorating the twenty-fifth anniversary of Pius's death. While boarding a plane for Rome, the former papal housekeeper collapsed at the Schwechat Airport, and though quickly hospitalized and given emergency treatment, she died a few days later. At the time of her death, she had been living in a home for elderly women in Rome named after Pius, which she had founded 14 years after the pope's death and where she had been working diligently as a key witness for the beatification and eventual sainthood of Pius XII.

How did Josefine Lehnert (Sister Pasqualina), a Bavarian farmer's daughter, meet the man who would one day become Pius XII?

Fräulein Lehnert had not yet reached her twenty-third birthday when she met Monsignor Eugenio Pacelli for the first time. He was just past 40 at the time and was well on the road to recovery from a prolonged illness while housed in a sanitorium on the Swiss side of Lake Constance, where Lehnert was a nun working on the wards. Monsignor Pacelli, then serving as the papal nuncio in Munich, was fluent in German, and had had many extended conversations with her: when he said he needed a housekeeper in the apostolic nunciature, the dedicated nun offered to take on the job. Pleased to no end, the monsignor made arrangements for her to be transferred.

She worked for Pacelli as a house servant and secretary in the Munich office, and when he was transferred to a more important assignment in Berlin, Sister Pasqualina, now 30 years old, went along—as she did again when Pacelli was made a cardinal in Rome and eventually appointed Vatican secretary of state by Pope Pius XI. In 1939, Sister Pasqualina went along with Pacelli when he was elected pontiff and became Pope Pius XII.

Although she and two other nuns from her order kept his household on the top floor of the Apostolic Palace, in the pope's office the petite Bavarian woman personally took care of almost every detail—like parceling out his writing paper and keeping his fountain pen filled. But it went much further than that: She took dictation from him every day, even writing pages in his private diary and editing his official papers and speeches. Pius often discussed critical matters with her, seeking her views on problems he had to address officially. And though he did not always see eye to eye with her, many times he changed his opinion to hers because he had such great faith in her intelligence, insight, and intuition. As the association went on, Pius was to engage Pasqualina more and more in his confidential work.

Quite often he would ask her to make telephone calls on his behalf and carry out papal visits in his name. Everyone in Rome knew that whenever Sister Pasqualina went alone somewhere in a Vatican car, she was on an errand of mercy at the behest of the Holy Father, often delivering cash gifts from the private funds of "Papa Pacelli" (as the Romans always called him) to some needy family or person.

The daily mail deliveries to the Vatican invariably contained a heavy pile of letters addressed directly to her, the majority of which were from Germany and Austria.

Although many of these letters were requests for funds or for a job within the Vatican, they also covered a wide range of subjects, such as petitions for church annulments for married but separated couples, grievances against curial politicians, and even requests for the pope's autograph. The writers were obviously aware that Pasqualina signified the best and most direct channel to the pope. Though she herself was a kind of secretary to the pontiff, the volume of mail she got each week would have justified her engaging her own private secretary; however, she never sought one and took care of all her own correspondence efficiently. She was a workhorse.

There were many other items of sensitive business that Pasqualina often handled for the pontiff. Facing daily problems involving the administration of the government of Vatican City, the nun never took on the decision-making role without consulting her mentor, though she had a lot to say on all complex matters. This was true in the case of the future Pope Paul VI, then Monsignor Montini, who was transferred to Milan in a move that surprised even most of the Vatican insiders; they knew, however, it had been orchestrated by Pasqualina. "La Popessa" did not like Montini at all and had frequently exchanged angry words with him, with Pius often having to intercede to smooth down one squabble or another. That Montini remained without a red hat while he was archbishop of Milan was another example of Pasqualina's influence that incensed many clerics at the Vatican. Not that anybody could ever support that accusation with hard evidence. But the talk persisted, as Archbishop Montini of Milan ran the second most powerful archdiocese in Italy sans the rank of cardinal.

On the other hand, Pasqualina had nothing but the highest esteem and admiration for Cardinal Spellman of New York, and though she may have applied protective restrictions to other ranking clergy who wanted to see the pope, she rolled out the red carpet for the American prelate. She had a special affection for the Irish priest, even though she had him accurately pegged as a calculating, conniving master politician eager to make friends in high places. Spellman owed his promotion to cardinal and to the job as archbishop of New York above all to Pasqualina. The pope had been undecided as to whom to name as head of the most important and influential archdiocese in the United States—Archbishop John T. McNicholas of Cincinnati or Bishop Spellman of Boston. McNicholas was the frontrunner in everybody's opinion, especially that of the New York press corps, which had written many feature stories on his imminent ascendancy to the post. Pasqualina made her opinion known to Pius during several chats with him; she suggested that because Spellman had excellent connections with President Roosevelt (not a matter for the Church to ignore at a time when the Vatican might need a direct pipeline into the White House) and he had demonstrated incredible fund-raising proclivities, he should be put in charge of New York. To what degree Pius's eventual decision to appoint Spellman to the job was in fact prompted by the urgings of his closest adviser, Sister Pasqualina, can never be determined, but not only did Spellman himself give her some of the credit, but just about everybody in the Vatican shared the same opinion.

One thing is known—the Sacred College of Cardinals was greatly upset that a pope could fall under so much womanly influence on such an important administrative matter, especially since the cardinals in the Curia had preferred McNicholas from the beginning. One of McNicholas's arch supporters was the all-powerful French cardinal Tisserant, with whom Pasqualina had feuded hotly and heavily for nearly two decades.

One day when Tisserant, accompanied by Monsignor Domenico Tardini, the Vatican pro-secretary of state, went to Pasqualina demanding to see the Holy Father immediately, Pasqualina would not let them into the office. Pounding the table in frustration, Tisserant raised his voice in an infuriated manner and insisted on seeing Pius. Calm as could be, Pasqualina picked up the phone and asked that the Swiss Guards rush an emergency squad to her office. Within half a minute two of them burst into the room, and Pasqualina boldly ordered them to escort the pair of high-ranking prelates out of the pontiff's antechamber. Understandably, the Swiss Guards were flabbergasted, but before the two startled clerics could be taken in hand by the spear-brandishing soldiers, the enraged Tisserant and equally enraged Tardini turned around and, muttering under their breath, stalked swiftly from the office.

Even more dismaying to Tisserant was the day he had an appointment with Pius on an urgent matter, and his appointment was canceled because Pasqualina had given the pope's time to Gary Cooper and Clare Boothe Luce, who were both in Rome for just a few hours. The dean of cardinals often had to wait up to 60 days before he could see the pope, simply because Pasqualina decreed it.

Another time she kept Bishop Angelo Roncalli (later to become Pope John XXIII) waiting for more than an hour while she gave priority to Clark Gable, then a major with the liberating American forces in Rome. The MGM star, who did not have a previous appointment, was allowed into the pope's office despite the fact that Roncalli had been summoned to the Vatican by Pius on a pressing matter. Both Pasqualina and Pius were known to be devoted fans of Gable (who, incidentally, was not a Roman Catholic).

Tisserant and Pasqualina had their final fallout an hour or so after the pope's death. Pius had entrusted to his confidante two large sacks of letters and memos that he said he wanted her to burn as soon as possible. This she did immediately. When Tisserant found out, moments after she had finished burning the personal and private papers, he raced into her office and lashed into her. Defending herself calmly, she observed that she had acted at the direct command of the Holy Father. In a fury Tisserant let her know that the papal documents included several handwritten first drafts of speeches Pius had planned to make, as well as notes and comments he had jotted down at his most recent private audiences.

During Pius's last months, when he was in very fragile health, Sister Pasqualina kept many of the Vatican's most important clerics, including Cardinal Tisserant, away from him if she suspected the pontiff would be upset or become unduly tired by the visit. She did this, unfortunately, far too often at a time when she also allowed the pope to receive large group audiences. Once she permitted a large body of newspaper vendors to visit with the pope on that same day that she postponed a meeting with Tisserant until the next morning.

Whenever a pope dies, there is an immediate total change of everything, down to the most minute detail. Upon Pius's death Pasqualina realized that she would no longer be working or residing in the Vatican and that she would need a place to live. She also knew she had too many enemies in Vatican City to expect help there. To the rescue, all the way from the Big Apple, came Cardinal Spellman, who, with his good connections at the pontifical North American College on Rome's Janiculum Hill, arranged for the German nun to take on some duties as a housekeeper there in exchange for room and board. As it worked out, Pasqualina never had to engage in any kind of household chores or other menial jobs, for she was immediately put to work on writing her reminiscences of the pope for the Vatican Library's collection of original manuscripts. Thanks to Spellman, she had been cocooned against Tisserant's venom, although on Pius's death, the bearded French prelate had dispatched an unranked priest to her chamber to inform her she had to leave the Vatican as soon as she could gather up her personal belongings.

When she walked out of the Apostolic Palace and

downstairs to St. Peter's Square to get into a taxicab with two valises and a birdcage housing a pair of Pius's pet canaries, not one priest or Vatican citizen came to wish "La Popessa" well, despite the fact that many of them had sought her favor in the past. Nobody even offered her help with the luggage.

The most powerful woman in Vatican history was 64 years old when the cab drove her off. Sister Pasqualina had done her job well— perhaps *too* well.

11. The Vatican's Swiss Guards

Tourists and pilgrims who swarm every year to Rome never overlook a chance to double-ogle the world's most picturesque army. Held in fascination by the masses who tour Rome during the big-draw months, the Swiss Guards are perhaps the world's most photographed soldiers— with nonstop cameras going clickety-split.

Brandishing seven-foot pikes or halberds, the men in those colorful uniforms who look like toy soldiers have the job of guarding the State of Vatican City and the pontiff who sits at its head. Truly, they comprise the most famous army in the world—and it's no small wonder that thousands upon thousands of tourists every week seek to have their picture taken alongside one of these papal protectors standing vigil at each of the three main entrances into the Vatican.

Apart from their stagelike duties in front of the public, the Guards patrol the Apostolic Palace corridor just outside the papal apartments 24 hours around the clock, and when the pope goes in or out, the uniformed sentinel on duty gives a snappy salute on bended knee. The Guards also do duty in the palace at Castel Gandolfo outside Rome where popes usually spend part of their summer months.

Some quickie questions now: What indeed is behind the pope's glamorous personal army? Are those men in the funny uniforms really trained professional soldiers— or just good-looking male models hired to wear the colorful garb as part of the sideshow activities to which St. Peter's Square is heir?

Initially, let's dispel one of the biggest myths of all about the Swiss Guards. Contrary to what most tourist guides tell visitors, the weird-looking uniform—with the slashed bouffant sleeves, striped doublet, and hose, all in gold, white, red, yellow and blue—was not designed by Michelangelo. Nor by Raffaello.

When Pope Benedict took over the papacy in 1914, he asked a Vatican seamstress to dream up suitable apparel for his soldiers from Switzerland; the woman surpassed herself in conceiving the ceremonial attire, and the pope so heartily approved that he adopted it immediately. Those puffy sleeves, however, do hark back to the middle of the sixteenth century, and, as nearly as can be determined, the unknown designer could quite possibly have been inspired by a Raffaello painting that shows similar suits of clothes, at that time the style in France.

Next question: What was the inspiration behind the establishment of the Swiss Guards? In the sixteenth century, Cardinal Giuliano della Rovere (the then Bishop of

Lausanne) was so impressed by Switzerland's soldiers that he advised Pope Sixtus IV to sign an alliance with some Swiss cantons. After the cardinal became Pope Julius II, he brought in 150 Swiss soldiers when the first stone of the new St. Peter's Basilica was laid in January 1506. That makes the Swiss Guards the oldest continuous military corps in existence.

Like other volunteer armies today, the Swiss Guards have a tough time finding enough recruits to keep their complement at 100. Recruits must be between 18 and 25 years of age, about 6 feet tall, and must sign a contract to serve a 2-year tour of duty. Most of the newcomers hardly ever reenlist, but a few do make it a career and stay on for as long as 30 years. The main problems are that the work is found monotonous, the discipline is apparently the toughest of any army anywhere, private life is almost impossible, the hours are very long, and duty is required every Sunday. Moreover, the pay is low.

In addition, the men are not permitted to marry during the first few years in the service. Nor are they allowed to bring any friends into their Vatican quarters for social visits. Most of their free time is given over to the required study of the Italian language and to special technical and commercial courses to prepare them for a future as civilians.

Sworn to protect the life of the pope at the risk of their own lives, the Swiss Guards narrowly escaped annihilation on the steps of St. Peter's during the sack of Rome on May 6, 1527, when 10,000 German and Spanish mercenaries in the pay of Emperor Charles V stormed the Vatican. Three quarters of the now-enlarged Swiss complement was destroyed—altogether 147 men—while the invaders, on the other hand, lost more than 800 soldiers. During the bloodletting battle, the commanding officer of the Guards, Colonel Gaspare Rouat, was killed in action. Seeing him fall mortally wounded, his wife picked up her husband's weapon and fought in his place until she—at the entrance to the basilica—died under enemy fire. The remaining 42 Swiss Guards enabled Pope Clement VII and 13 of his cardinals to flee to safety along Vatican ramparts into the impregnable Castel Sant'Angelo fortress.

Since that 1527 slaughter, the Swiss Guards have never again had to fight any battles, but on several occasions the Guards had to lay down their arms on papal orders, rather than face extermination. This was even true when Napoleon invaded Rome and carried the pope off to France.

In World War II, Pope Pius XII made the guards store away their firearms (all guns were later abolished by Pope Paul VI in 1970), so they patrolled the frontier between the State of Vatican City and Italy with only their combination spear-battleaxes while facing Nazi Germany's array of Panzer tanks, which never once dared to cross the border without a direct order from Hitler. It was one of World War II's most curious sights to see the heavily armed Nazi troops stand by rather sheepishly as a lone Swiss Guard patrolled up and down with a hand weapon from the bygone days. After Joe Stalin heard about the solitary Swiss Guard keeping Hitler's army at bay—so the story goes—he shook his head in disbelief and asked: "So, tell me, how many divisions does the pope have?"

Another story that Guards like to tell about their corps is the one about the coronation of Clement XIII in 1758. On that occasion, some Swiss Guards turned away a Franciscan friar who did not seem to them to fit in with all the cardinals and dignitaries on hand. Eleven years later, after that same quondom friar had been crowned Pope Clement XIV, the Franciscan said: "I enjoyed this coronation. This time the Swiss Guards let me in!"

Appendix II

Glossary of Vatican Terminology

Aggiornamento: An Italian word referring to a renewal or revitalization of institutional reform and change in the Church

Archdiocese: An ecclesiastical territory and jurisdiction governed by an archbishop

Beatification: A preliminary step toward sainthood

Bull: An apostolic bull is a papal document dealing with an important subject, to which has been attached a lead seal called a *bulla*. The lead seal is embossed on one side with the signature of the pope.

Canon law: A body of Church laws, in the sense of regulating norms

Canonization: A declaration by the pope that a person who died as a martyr and/or practiced Christian virtues to a heroic degree is in heaven

Concordat: A church-state treaty with the force of law, having to do with matters of mutual concern

Consistory: An assembly of cardinals presided over by the pope

Crypt: An underground chamber, often used for burial or worship

Curia: The administrative body of cardinals through which the pope governs

Diocese: An organized ecclesiastic territory under the direction of a bishop

Encyclical: A letter issued by the pope that treats a matter of grave or timely importance and is intended for extensive circulation

Friar: Member of a mendicant order, as distinguished from a member of a monastic order

Holy See: (1) The Diocese of Rome; (2) The pope himself and/or officials and bodies of the Church's central administration at Vatican City

Index: A now-defunct list of prohibited books that Catholics were forbidden to read

Miracles: An observable event in the physical world that cannot be explained by natural laws and that is therefore classified by Church officialdom as an act of God

Monk: A member of a monastic order who binds himself to a religious profession and lives in a monastery

Monsignor: A title of distinction granted to a priest as a mark of papal recognition

Nun: A member of a religious order of women who take solemn vows; these women are often called "sisters"

Peter's Pence: A worldwide collection made each year among Catholics and used by the pope in administering his charities

Relics: The physical remains and effects of saints, which are considered worthy of veneration

Rota: A Church court that decides on marriage annulment cases

Saint: A holy person who has died and is declared a saint by the Church hierarchy; he or she is considered living in heaven with God

See: Another word for diocese or archdiocese; it is the jurisdiction of a bishop

Sister: Any woman who has taken religious vows and lives in a convent

Synod: Meeting of priests and other persons of a diocese to take action on matters concerning the clergy and the faithful

Temporal power: The right of the pope to hold and govern territory

Vow: A promise made to God

Zucchetto: A skullcap worn by bishops and other prelates

Appendix III

Significant Dates in Catholic Church History

A.D. **64 or 67** : Peter is crucified and buried on Vatican Hill

324: Emperor Constantine's basilica honoring Peter is consecrated

452: Pope Saint Leo persuades Attila the Hun to spare Rome

848: Pope Leo IV decides to build a wall around Vatican property (hence the name Leonine Walls)

1059: The Lateran Council issues new legislation regarding papal elections; the voting power is entrusted to Roman cardinals

1226: Saint Francis of Assisi dies

1309: Pope Clement V elected; he decides to take up residence in Avignon (in what is now France), thereby beginning a line of popes who lived in Avignon until 1377

1377: Pope Gregory XI decides to leave Avignon and go to Rome to live

1424: Pope Nicholas V moves the government of the Church from the Lateran Palace to the Vatican

1626: The new St. Peter's Basilica, built over the first one erected by Constantine, is consecrated

1870: When recognition is not given papal temporal possessions and papal sovereignty by Italy, Pope Pius IX makes himself a virtual prisoner in the Vatican

1917: Apparitions of the Virgin Mary are reported at Fátima (Portugal)

1929: Treaty of the Lateran Pacts between Italy and the pope is signed, thereby creating a new country—the State of Vatican City

1958: Following the death of Pius XII, the reign of Pope John XXIII begins

1978: Polish Cardinal Karol Wojtyla is elected pope, the first non-Italian pontiff in over 455 years. He assumed the name John Paul II

1981: Pope John Paul II is severely wounded by gunshots in an assassination attempt in St. Peter's Square

About the Author

Except for five years spent teaching sociology and anthropology at the University of Kansas, Nino Lo Bello was a journalist all his adult life. While stationed in Rome, Mr. Lo Bello covered Italy for the *New York Herald Tribune* for eight years and was a special correspondent for the *International Herald Tribune* for more than a quarter of a century. Lo Bello is the author of ten books, among them *The Vatican Empire, Vatican U.S.A., European Detours, The Vatican Papers, Nino Lo Bello's Guide to Offbeat Europe,* and *Nino Lo Bello's Guide to the Vatican.* An incurable opera buff, for nearly three decades Lo Bello syndicated radio interviews with opera stars singing in Europe.

Born in New York City (Brooklyn) and educated at Queens College and New York University, Mr. Lo Bello came from an Italian immigrant family. He was a member of the Overseas Press Club of America and has served on the board of directors of Vienna's Foreign Press Club. He won a number of awards for his work as a writer, the latest one being from the Federal Republic of Austria—a silver medal to honor his many articles dealing with Vienna and Austria over a 25-year period. Mr. Lo Bello was married to a former New York editor (Irene Rooney Lo Bello), and they are the parents of two grown children, Susan and Tom.